The Iron Horse

The first railroad to cross the Allegheny Mountains in the early 1850s. Riding in front are railroad employees and their families.

The Iron Horse

How Railroads Changed America

Richard Wormser

Walker and Company
New York

First published in the United States of America in 1993 by Walker
Publishing Company, Inc.

Published simultaneously in Canada by Thomas Allen & Son Canada,
Limited, Markham, Ontario

Library of Congress Cataloging-in-Publication Data
Wormser, Richard, 1933–
The iron horse : how railroads changed America / Richard Wormser.
p.   cm.
Includes bibliographical references and index.
Summary: Traces the history of railroads, how they helped shape
America, their symbolism, accidents and safety problems,
technological advances, and disputes between railroad magnates and
workers.
ISBN 0-8027-8221-3   ISBN 0-8027-8222-1   (lib. bdg.)
1. Railroads—United States—Juvenile literature.   [1. Railroads—
History.]   I. Title.
TF23.W67   1993
385′.0973—dc20   93-12128
CIP
AC

Except where noted, all illustrations appear courtesy of
the Library of Congress.

Book Design by Claire Vaccaro

Printed in the United States of America

2   4   6   8   10   9   7   5   3   1

To Elsie, who helped me find the right track.

Contents

The Iron Horse

A drawing showing the race between the horse Lightning and the steam engine Tom Thumb *in 1830. The horse won the race when the engine broke down.*

1
The Iron Horse Comes to America

"Teakettle on a truck"

The odds were on the horse.

The year was 1830. The race was between a gray mare named Lightning and a steam locomotive called *Tom Thumb,* named after a famous circus midget of the day. Each pulled a carriage filled with passengers. Five thousand people had gathered outside Baltimore, Maryland, to see whether this new mechanical wonder, invented by Peter Cooper of New York, could travel faster than the fastest of domestic animals. Most believed the engine to be little more than a toy to amuse children and frighten women.

At high noon, the horse and one-ton steam locomotive lined up side by side, the locomotive on its tracks, the horse and carriage on the ground alongside. The crowd grew quiet as the starter raised his gun, counted to three, and fired. They were off and running, the locomotive spewing black smoke and glowing sparks, the horse panting and snorting. John Latrobe, an eyewitness to the event, reported what happened next:

The Iron Horse

The horse had pulled perhaps a quarter of a mile ahead when the safety valve of the engine lifted and a thin, blue vapor issuing from it showed as an excess of steam. The blower whistled, the steam blew off in vaporizing clouds; the passengers shouted; it was neck and neck, nose and nose. Then the engine passed the horse and a great hurrah hailed the victory. Just at that time, as the gray mare was giving up, the band slipped from the pulley of the boiler . . . and the engine began to wheeze and putt. The horse gained on the machine and passed it and although the band was replaced and the steam engine did its best, the horse was too far ahead to be overtaken and came in the winner of the race. But the real victor was Mr. Cooper, notwithstanding.

Many people laughed and shook their heads and told Mr. Cooper that his "teakettle on a truck" had no future. But for those who were in tune with nineteenth-century America, there was no question which way the future would head.

By 1830, America was on the verge of a transportation revolution. For almost two hundred years stagecoaches, wagons, and boats were the major means of moving people and goods. Progress had been slow at first, because roads and canals had to be built from scratch. When the first English immigrants waded ashore on the coasts of Virginia and New England in the early seventeenth century, they confronted a land that one Pilgrim grimly described as "a howling wilderness." Filled with dense forests, boulders, swamps, and mountains, it was almost impassable. The only paths were Indian trails. The only means of river travel was by canoe. Before there could be vehicles to transport goods and people, roads had to be built. As the colonies grew, a network of roads gradually evolved, connecting town to town and eventually city to city. And once the roads were built, horse-drawn vehicles like stagecoaches and wagons could be used to transport people and goods. Eventually, a system of private roads called turnpikes was developed. Tolls were charged for passengers and vehicles depending on how much distance one traveled. In principle, the private turnpikes were exactly like the public ones of today.

The first stagecoaches were crude vehicles without springs that provided little comfort. A hapless passenger would be bounced and joggled throughout the journey as the coach shook, rattled, and rolled over the rough roads. In the express coaches that traveled between major cities, passengers spent nineteen hours a day traveling and were allowed only four hours' sleep a night. The coach stopped periodically at rest stations for the driver to change horses and for passengers to stretch their legs, eat a meal that usually seemed likely to poison them, and, if it was night, sleep in beds or on the floor while bugs dined on them. If an axle broke or a wheel rolled off, the passengers would get out and wait until repairs were made. If the hill was too steep for the horses to climb, the passengers would carry their luggage so the empty stagecoach could get to the top. If a coach got stuck in the mud or a ditch, the passengers pushed and pulled the vehicle until it was back on the road. When a stagecoach traveled over a road with deep ruts, it was not unusual for the driver to turn around and shout to the passengers inside to lean one way or another to balance the coach and keep it upright. "Now, gentlemen, to the right!" he would call out, followed by "Now, gentlemen, to the left!"—depending upon which direction the coach was in danger of tipping over.

On poor roads, a six-team stagecoach could average two miles an hour, on good roads, eight miles; if the driver was really moving, he could make ten miles an hour.

The Iron Horse

By the nineteenth century, stagecoaches had become the main means of overland travel in America, with as many as twenty coaches a day running between large cities. As more people traveled, both roads and stagecoaches were improved to provide a comfortable and pleasant way to journey. The better stagecoaches were supported by metal springs, which gave the vehicle a pleasant riding motion and prevented the violent rocking that sometimes injured passengers. Luggage was now stored on the roof rather than under the seats, and most coaches held nine passengers rather than the twelve that many earlier stagecoaches had. The better stagecoaches also had windows, rather than mere curtain-covered openings in the side.

As stagecoaches improved, so did wagons, which were the most common way of carrying goods from one place to another and transporting people emigrating to the West. One of the most famous wagons of the eighteenth and nineteenth centuries was the Conestoga wagon, named after the town in Pennsylvania where it was made, which carried people to the far West during the gold rush days. These sturdy wagons, which weighed three quarters of a ton, were called "prairie schooners," because they looked like boats sailing across the open lands of the Great Plains. But wagon travel was slow. In 1756 it took three days to make the ninety-mile trip between Philadelphia and New York.

Boats were another means of transportation used in early America. The Indians taught the first settlers how to make canoes. In time, boats became more sophisticated; by the nineteenth century there were a variety of barges, flatboats, rafts, keelboats, and schooners traveling up and down rivers and across lakes. Small boats drifted down rivers with the current; to move them upstream, the crew pushed long poles against the river bottom. Larger boats had sails and were propelled by the wind.

A wagon train of pioneers headed west in the 1860s.

The Iron Horse

Canals connected one body of water to another, allowing boats to transport passengers and freight hundreds of miles without ever touching land. One of the great canals of the nineteenth century was the Erie Canal in New York, which began at Lake Erie and ended in Albany. It was 363 miles long, forty feet wide, and four feet deep, and cost $13 million to build. In some canals, boats were towed by horses walking on a path alongside the canal. Canal travel enabled a large number of goods and people to be transported over a long distance inexpensively. But canals had many problems. They froze in winter, and even in good weather they were often closed for repairs or because there was too much or too little water in them due to floods or droughts.

Most people put up with the inconveniences of travel, as there were no alternatives. But there were a few visionaries who dreamed of newer and better ways to journey on both land and water. The steam engine had been invented in England in the eighteenth century, and experiments had been successfully carried out in Europe using steam as a means of propulsion. In the late eighteenth century, an American by the name of John Fitch invented a design for a steamboat, but most people laughed at him. He presented his vision to anyone who would listen—including Benjamin Franklin, who, in addition to his many political accomplishments, was also the foremost inventor of his day. Franklin listened respectfully to what Fitch had to say, and then offered Fitch a small sum of money—implying it was for charity rather than an investment. Fitch was furious. He refused to take any money for his personal needs but angrily told Franklin that if he wished, he could become a subscriber to the project.

Fitch was a driven man, and his persistence eventually paid off. He did raise enough money to build a working steamboat, but he was years ahead of his time. His idea never caught on and Fitch finally gave up his dream and went to live in the then wilderness of Kentucky.

It was up to Robert Fulton to pick up where Fitch left off. He, too, dreamed of a steamboat and also met resistance and ridicule. Like Fitch, he persisted with his dream; but unlike Fitch, Fulton eventually triumphed. In 1807 people were astounded to see a steam-powered boat called the *Clermont* travel up the Hudson River from New York City to Albany, a journey of 160 miles. A young boy by the name of Henry Freeland witnessed the event and its effect on those who saw it:

> Some imagined it to be a sea monster while others didn't hesitate to express their belief that it might be the sign of the approaching (last) judgement. What seemed strange in the vessel was the substitution of lofty and straight smoke-stacks rising from the decks instead of gracefully topped masts that commonly stand on vessels to navigate the stream. . . .
>
> The whole country talked of nothing but a sea monster belching forth fire and smoke. The fishermen were terrified and saw nothing but destruction devastating their fishing grounds. . . . Yet, who could doubt that Fulton saw the world navigated by steam and that his invention was car-rying the message of freedom to every land? . . . What a wonderful achievement! What a splendid triumph!

Within a few decades steamboats were used throughout America. They traveled up and down the Hudson, Mississippi, Missouri, and Ohio rivers, carrying passengers and freight, providing entertainment and excitement (usually gambling and dance-hall girls), and becoming

Representation of Robert Fulton's steamboat Clermont *making its first voyage up the Hudson River in 1807.*

part of the American legend. It was, according to Mark Twain, also the dream of every young boy at that time to become a steamboat pilot: "When I was a boy, there was one permanent ambition among our comrades in my village on the west bank of the Mississippi. That was, to be a steamboat man."

There were some who believed that what worked well on water might work even better on land. In 1804, Oliver Evans, who was considered an eccentric by his neighbors, petitioned the Pennsylvania legislature for the right to use state highways for a "wagon propelled by steam." The legislature debated on whether or not he should be classified as insane but decided to grant him the privilege on the grounds that it would not cause any harm.

Evans had invented a combination steam car and boat rolled into one. He named it *Orukter Amphibolus,* and drove it over the cobble-stoned streets of Philadelphia and into the nearby Schuylkill River, where it was propelled by paddles. He also believed he could build what he called a "steam wagon," that is, a locomotive pulling "carriages" that would travel on a wooden track at a rate of fifteen miles an hour. Before his death in 1819, he predicted: "I do verily believe that carriages propelled by steam will come into general use and travel at the rate of 300 miles a day."

About the same time, a man named John Stevens, who was then seventy-two years old and a great believer in steam-powered travel, constructed a working locomotive that ran on tracks he had built on his estate. It was perhaps the largest toy train that the world has ever seen. He believed that it could serve as the model for a railroad. But, like Evans, Stevens was ahead of his time.

Actually, railways had been operating in England since the eighteenth century. In fact, the English were so afraid of America learning about steam-powered locomotives that it was considered a crime for anyone in England to inform Americans how they worked. The penalty was a year in prison and a fine of about $1,000. The reason for the fear was that English merchants were aware that America, despite being a young country, had the potential to be a serious economic rival. Many of England's most skilled industrial mechanics had immigrated to the United States to work for American companies, which not only paid better wages, but offered better working conditions.

In 1830, the year that Peter Cooper's locomotive lost to the horse named Lightning, several railroads had already begun operations. A train in Charleston, South Carolina, was the first steam-driven locomotive in America to carry passengers. Called the *Best Friend of Charleston*, the locomotive traveled a distance of six miles. Like all early locomotives, the *Best Friend of Charleston* burned wood and carried a crew consisting of an engineer who drove the train, a fireman who fueled the boiler, and a conductor who collected fares. It was also the first train to have an accident, which occurred when the fireman, bothered by a noisy safety valve, decided to sit on it to keep it quiet. The pressure built up inside the boiler until it exploded, sending both the boiler and the fireman flying through the air. The fireman died from his injuries, thus becoming the first railroad fatality in America. By the end of the year, a total of forty miles of track had been laid down in America. By 1835, slightly more than a thousand miles of track had been built.

In the early days of railroads, riding a train was an adventure, if not a nightmare. Schedules were unreliable. People never knew what time a train would depart or when it would arrive. In 1850, for example, a traveler made a record of a trip he took in New York State between Albany and Buffalo, which, according to the railroad sched-

A model of the Best Friend of Charleston, *the first steam locomotive to carry passengers in America in 1830.*

ule, was a journey of fourteen hours. The following is a log of that "fourteen-hour" journey.

Saturday, 8 P.M.	Train departs Albany.
Saturday, 11:30 P.M.	Train arrives in Utica. Sits on a siding for three hours which neither conductor nor crew can explain.
Sunday, 2:00 A.M.	Train leaves Utica.
Sunday, 5:00 A.M.	Train arrives Syracuse. Remains in Syracuse for more than twelve hours. Conductor and crew neither know or care why.
Sunday, 5:30 P.M.	Train leaves Syracuse.
Monday, 12:00 A.M.	Train arrives in Rochester. Sits six hours waiting for proper locomotive.
Monday, 1:30 P.M.	Train arrives in Buffalo.

The total time for the trip was thirty-nine and a half hours and the total distance was 290 miles!

Once on board, passengers had to be prepared for anything to happen. The first coaches were attached to one another by chains. Whenever the locomotive started, it would jerk the passengers forward and then throw them backward, knocking off men's hats and sometimes throwing passengers to the floor. Passengers also risked having their clothes burned off their backs by the sparks escaping from the train's smokestack.

If the train ran low on wood for the boiler, then the passengers might have to jump out and chop down a few trees. If a train jumped the tracks, the passengers would help put it back on. There was no ventilation in the early carriages, and the only way to get fresh air—and a faceful of soot, ashes, and sparks—was to open a window or side panel. Nor did passenger coaches have any of the comforts that we take for granted today. They lacked bathrooms, drinking water, sleeping berths, and comfortable seats. The only light at night was provided by two candles stuck at each end of the coach (a total of four candles). Food was not served on board and when a train stopped at a station for a few minutes, the passengers dashed out, swallowed whatever they could find, and rushed back before the train left them behind. To keep passengers warm in winter, railroad cars usually had a stove at one end of each car. Those who sat next to the stove usually perspired, while those seated in the car's center or its far end froze. However, if there was an accident, those seated next to the stove were often fatally burned.

Passengers were not the only ones unhappy with the early railroads. Stagecoach and boat companies tried their best to sabotage them to prevent competition. Farmers were angry because trains frightened their livestock, caused their horses to run away, spread soot and ashes over their laundry, and set fire to their homes and fields with flying sparks and cinders. Trains were constantly running over cows and other farm animals that wandered onto the track. Occasionally an angry bull charged a locomotive, knocking the train off its track. Some farmers became so annoyed with the railroads' killing their livestock that they fired shotguns at the engines as they passed. Eventually, one Isaac Dripp invented a cowcatcher, which was an iron skirt in front of the train that pushed the cow off the track and out of the train's path. The cowcatcher had prongs or spikes in front of it.

MORE PLUCKY THAN PRUDENT.

A caricature of a common problem in the early days of railroading—a bull on the tracks. Notice the cowcatcher in front of the train. This grille was designed to push the animal off the track and soften the impact of collision.

The first time it was used, it struck a bull, impaling the poor animal on the spikes. It took a block and tackle to pull the bull off. After that, Dripp installed a guard around the spikes so that the animal would be pushed off the tracks rather than speared.

A few farmers saw a chance to make money out of the railroad's accidental killing of animals. They would place their oldest animals on the track to be run over by a train; then they would demand that the railroad pay them full market value. At first, many railroads did so, not wanting to antagonize the farmers. But when a railroad in Michigan began to draw the line and stated that from then on, it would pay only half the market value, the farmers revolted. They began to harass the railroad by putting oil on the rails, throwing sand into machinery, and placing logs and boulders on the tracks to derail the trains. When the railroad refused to yield, the farmers threw rocks at the trains and fired at passengers and engineers. The railroad struck back. Officials sent spies to infiltrate the farmers to learn who their leaders were. Then, one night, seventy-five detectives arrested thirty-six men, eleven of whom were sent to jail.

A number of people objected to the railroad on religious grounds, seeing it as a product of the devil and against God. One legislator condemned it from the floor of the state assembly:

> The railroad stems from Hell. It is the Devil's own invention . . . spreading its infernal poison throughout the countryside. . . . It will set fire to houses along its slimy tracks. . . . It will leave the land despoiled . . . a desert where only buzzards shall wing their loathsome way to feed upon carrion accomplished by the iron monster of the locomotive engine . . . let us hear no more of the railroad.

One minister thundered against it from his pulpit by reviling it as "an odious and monstrous violation, not only of the laws of God, but of all decencies in a Christian Society."

Railroads often got a bad name from stock speculators, who sometimes sold worthless stock to an unsuspecting public. To build a railroad cost a great deal of money, and railroad builders sold stocks and bonds to raise the funds they needed. In those days, there was no regulation of stock transactions and many devious promoters sold stocks in nonexistent railroad companies to unsuspecting people. "Worthless as railroad stock" was a common saying of the time to describe something as having absolutely no value.

It was accidents, however, that gave railroads their worst reputation. Between 1853 and 1859, there were over 900 railroad accidents (called concussions), causing 1,109 deaths. Many accidents were caused by stupidity, carelessness, and drunkenness. In Connecticut, an engineer failed to see that a drawbridge over a river was open; he drove the train over it and into the water, at a cost of forty-two lives. In Illinois, two railroads claimed the right of way at a crossing they shared in common. Each operated its trains as if the other did not exist. When the inevitable happened and two trains crashed, eighteen people were killed. Even the president of the United States was not immune to railroad tragedy. In 1847 President Franklin Pierce and his wife were horrified to see their sole surviving son, eleven years old, killed in a railroad accident before their eyes.

Poorly constructed bridges caused many railroad tragedies. Often bridges were too flimsy to bear the weight of trains that passed over them. In New York, a bridge collapsed as a train crossed over it and the last two cars fell forty feet into the river below. Forty-nine people died.

But despite the complaints, frauds, inconveniences, and tragedies, railroads mushroomed all over the eastern United States. By 1850, 9,000 miles of railroad track in America had been constructed in the twenty-five states east of the Mississippi River. By 1860, there were over 30,000 miles of track, and railroads were laying down another 2,500 miles more each year. There was more railroad construction in the United States than there was in the rest of the world combined. The American economy was booming. There was prosperity everywhere, and people were looking for new markets for their goods. Farmers along the upper Mississippi wanted to sell their wheat and produce to the major cities of the East. Southern cotton planters wanted to ship cotton to the seaports of New York and New England, where it could be shipped to Europe. Manufacturers in the Middle Atlantic states wanted to sell their products to the people of the West and South. Speculators and investors wanted to make money. Henry Thoreau caught the mood of the country when he wrote: "When I hear the Iron Horse make the hills echo with his snort like thunder, shaking the earth with his feet and breathing fire and smoke from his nostrils, it seems as if the earth had sent a race now worthy to inhabit it."

For both better and worse, the railroad became the symbol of the age. It touched a deep emotional chord in the American people, with "its power, the thrust of its great wheels, the clouds of trailing smoke, the tolling bell, the eerie whistle borne mournfully on the wind (the most haunting music of the age); greed at the wealth it promised; rage at its dictatorial and unpredictable ways and at the corruption that followed everywhere like a dark cloud."

Caricature of Commodore Cornelius Vanderbilt, the railroad king, holding two puppets on a string. The puppets represent Daniel Drew and Jay Gould. The drawing is meant to show that Vanderbilt was powerful enough to control Drew and Gould, even though they owned railroads themselves.

2
Railroad Builders and Barons

"His touch is death"

Most of the men who built America's railroads were rogues and scoundrels. Under today's laws, they would have been sent to prison. But the nineteenth-century industrialists—or robber barons, as they were called—could get away with murder and often did. They ruined their competitors and the lives of thousands of innocent people in their obsessive pursuit of wealth and power. The robber barons lied, cheated, and bribed state and federal legislators, governors, and judges. They created their own private armies, enforced their own laws, and brutally suppressed protest. For almost forty years after the Civil War, the industrialists, especially the railroad kings, were a law unto themselves. Few of them were interested in building railroads for their own sake or in bringing material benefits to the country, even though this often happened as a result of their activity. They were much more interested in turning the railroads into private money machines by manipulating the value of their stocks and bonds to make their fortunes—even if it meant ruining their companies. Their power was enormous. Lord Bryce, an English historian who visited the United States during the 1860s, noted in his book *The American Commonwealth*:

> These railway kings are . . . the greatest men in America. They have more power . . . than perhaps anyone in American political life, except the President [of the United States] who keeps [his] power only for four years while the railroad monarch may keep his for life.

One of the chief rogues was Cornelius Vanderbilt, called the Commodore because he had made his fortune in shipping before becoming involved in railroads. He was one of the first robber barons, a man without conscience who would destroy anyone who stood in his way. Once, when he thought a group of his associates cheated him, he sent them a brief note that read:

> Gentlemen:
>   You have undertaken to cheat me. I will not sue you for the law takes too long. I will ruin you.

He kept his word and bankrupted them.

Vanderbilt, the richest man in 1860 America, was the son of a poor man who operated a ferry. Like many people born to poverty, Vanderbilt had a fierce desire to become rich. Unlike most, however, he actually did so. Starting out as a ferryboat operator, Vanderbilt worked his way up in the shipping business until he owned his own fleet of ships. He lived in a simple house which was reported to contain rooms full of worn-out furniture. He allowed his family very little spending money. His long-suffering wife, Sophia, bore him nine children, most of whom he regarded as "idiots." When she finally had a mental breakdown, Vanderbilt placed her in an insane asylum and began to actively chase younger women.

In 1862, Vanderbilt, then sixty-eight years old, turned his incredible energy to railroads. He battled for and acquired two small New York City railroads, the Hudson and the New York and Harlem lines. The New York and Harlem was the only railroad that connected Albany, the capital of New York, with New York City. Then Vanderbilt turned his attention to larger game—the New York Central Railroad, which ran its trains between Buffalo and Albany.

Because it lacked a rail connection between Albany and New York, the New York Central used boats on the Hudson River to transport passengers who needed to travel between the two cities. Only in the wintertime, when the river was frozen, did the Central arrange for its passengers to take Vanderbilt's train.

This annoyed Vanderbilt. He wanted the Central to use his trains throughout the year. The New York Central curtly refused Vanderbilt's request. That was a big mistake, for Vanderbilt was not a man to be treated with disrespect. He said nothing but waited for his revenge. He would take advantage of the fact that both his line and that of the New York Central arrived and departed from the same depot in Albany, making it possible for passengers and freight to be transferred from one line to the other in a few minutes.

The following winter, without warning, Vanderbilt's trains suddenly stopped two miles outside of Albany instead of at the depot in the city! This meant that all the passengers and freight now had to be transported two miles in the snow and cold to the connecting New York Central train.

A roar of protest was heard throughout New York. Vanderbilt was criticized by the press and was summoned before an investigating committee of the New York State legislature. He was asked how he dared to inconvenience passengers by making them walk two miles in the bitter cold to change trains. Vanderbilt calmly listened to the legislators blow off steam.

> "Why, Mr. Vanderbilt," one legislator demanded, "did you not run the trains across the river as you used to?"
> "I was not there, gentlemen," he replied, implying that others gave the orders.
> "But what did you do when you heard of it?"
> "I did not do anything."
> "Why not? Where were you?"
> "I was at home playing a rubber of whist [a card game] and I never allow anything to interfere with me when I am playing that game. It requires, as you know, undivided attention."

Vanderbilt then played his trump card. He respectfully reminded the legislators that, at the New York Central's request, they had passed a law that prohibited any other railroad from entering Albany. Technically, Vanderbilt was right. The New York Central had persuaded—and probably bribed—the legislature to pass the law in order to prevent competition. In reality, the law was no longer enforced and the New York and Harlem train had been entering Albany for years. But the railroad and the state legislature knew when they were beaten. The New York Central's directors decided it was easier to join Vanderbilt rather than fight him. They sold him their railroad.

Few were a match for Vanderbilt, but there were three who were tough enough, mean enough, and dishonest enough to gain an advantage over him. They were Daniel Drew, Jay Gould, and Jim

Fisk, an unholy trinity of rascals if there ever was one. All grew up in poverty and clawed their way to the top. Drew, despite the fact that he was a deeply religious man, was a crook and an alcoholic. He would alternate between moments of piety and thievery, abstinence and alcoholism. He trusted no one and would ruin anyone given the chance.

Drew began his working life as a cattle drover, buying cattle on credit and then selling them at a distant market, sometimes not bothering to pay the original owner. That was the least of his deceptions. His most famous trick during this period of his life worked as follows: As he drove his stock of cattle to market, Drew refused to allow them to drink. The poor animals were so thirsty that when Drew finally let them drink just before he sold them, they swallowed enormous quantities of water—which, of course, added weight to them. Since cattle were sold by the pound, Drew made a good profit by selling his bloated cattle to unsuspecting buyers. The cattle would quickly lose the water weight they gained, but by that time the sale had been made and nothing could be done about it. This practice earned Drew a reputation for "watering stock," filling up his cattle with water to make them appear to be worth more than they

Portrait of Daniel Drew, one of Vanderbilt's fiercest rivals, who died penniless.

really were. Later on, Drew applied this same principle of "watering stock" to another kind of stock—the paper stocks of companies he owned. He would print stock with a total face value greater than the company's real worth and sell it on the market in the same way a counterfeiter prints false dollar bills and passes them off as real ones.

Another dirty trick Drew used was to go to the stock market and pretend to let a piece of paper fall out of his pocket without noticing it. On the paper was written the name of a stock that Drew was seemingly going to buy. Drew would always make sure that someone saw him drop the paper so that they would pick it up. Within a short time, everyone would be buying the stock named on Drew's paper, thinking they had an inside tip. What Drew actually wanted to do was to *sell* the stock—but at as high a price as possible. By creating a buying rush, Drew would make millions by secretly selling at the artificially high prices, while those who bought would lose large sums of money.

Drew's partners, Jay Gould and Jim Fisk, were as dishonest as he was. Jay Gould was perhaps the hardest man of all the robber barons of the period. He would betray anyone to make a profit. He was a lonely, bitter man, without friends, pity, patriotism, or compassion. He had a hard life as a child, working like a slave on a farm for his father. He had to beg his father to allow him to attend school. Gould was determined that he would not be a farmer. By the time he was sixteen, he had made his first business transaction, cheating someone on a land deal to make a profit. His career was launched. He was such a heartless man, with a tendency to destroy everything that he became involved in, that Daniel Drew remarked of him, "His touch is death!"

The third member of this "gang" was Jim Fisk. Fisk began his business career as a peddler, traveling around the country with his father, cheating farmers and their wives. He was a magnificent con artist who always put on an elaborate show before he made his sale. Fisk soon gave up peddling to become a promoter, involving himself in a thousand and one deals, profiting from them all until finally he began to do business with Drew and Gould.

Fisk was a big man with blond hair and a curling mustache. He dressed in fine clothes and gold rings and loved to spend his money on wine, women, and song. He fell in love with a beautiful actress of sorts named Josie Mansfield and made her his mistress. Fisk bought her a town house and, true to his generous nature, spent hundreds of thousands of dollars for her jewelry and clothes. Fisk abandoned his wife for Josie and proudly escorted her everywhere.

In the 1860s, a great railroad war broke out between Vanderbilt on one side and Drew, Fisk, and Gould on the other. At stake was control of the Erie Railroad. Drew controlled the stock of the Erie, a line that competed with Vanderbilt's New York Central Railroad for the Chicago market. Vanderbilt tried to buy a controlling block of Erie stock, and Drew pretended to cooperate by selling. But Drew had no intention of letting Vanderbilt control the Erie. Aided by Fisk and Gould, Drew came up with a scheme to illegally print additional stock and sell it on the market without revealing where it was coming from. Thus, every time Vanderbilt thought he had bought control of the Erie, more stock would mysteriously appear out of nowhere. Vanderbilt ordered his stockbroker to "Buy Erie. I don't care at what price. Just buy it!" The result was that the price of the stock rose every time Vanderbilt came close to cornering the market, and then dropped every time Drew, Fisk, and Gould printed a new batch. The scheme cost Vanderbilt millions of dollars and allowed Drew, Fisk, and Gould to make millions.

When Vanderbilt finally found out what his opponents were doing, he was furious. He had one of the judges he controlled declare the newly printed stocks illegal. But Fisk, Gould, and Drew always managed to find new ways to print more Erie stock. When Vanderbilt moved to have them arrested, the trio fled to New Jersey and continued to print more stock. Gould also bribed the New York State legislature to make his stock legal.

At the same time, both the New York Central Railroad and the Erie were engaged in a rate war with each other over the cost of transporting freight and passengers. When one railroad lowered its prices, the other responded by dropping its prices even lower. The goal was to drive the other railroad into bankruptcy, leaving the victor without competition and free to raise the rates as high as he wanted. At one point, both Vanderbilt and Fisk lowered the shipping rates of cattle on their respective lines to less than $1 a head. Fisk then secretly bought a large number of cattle and shipped them on Vanderbilt's line, making a large profit by doing so.

Finally, having had enough of the war, Vanderbilt sent Drew a message. "Drew. I'm sick of the whole damned business. Come and see me." Both sides met and at first called each other names. Gould called Vanderbilt a robber and told him that he had brought the punishment on himself. Vanderbilt threatened to keep his lawyers after the three of them until he got his money back no matter how long it would take or how much it would cost. But ultimately Vanderbilt was willing to settle because, as he pointed out, "It never pays to kick a skunk." Finally they came to an agreement. Drew, Gould, and Fisk agreed to pay Vanderbilt four and a half million dollars. In return Vanderbilt would withdraw his lawsuits and give up his fight to control the Erie. Both sides called a truce to the rate war. In the end, Vanderbilt's battle cost him about a million and a half dollars and he had nothing to show for it.

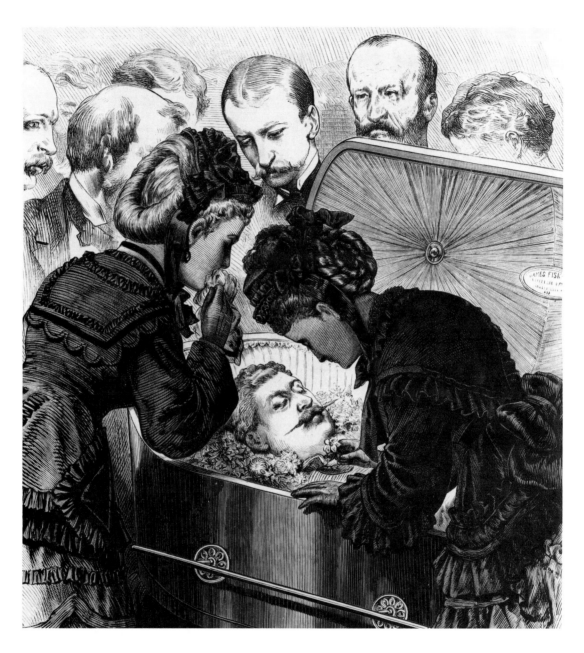

Caricature of the funeral of Jim Fisk, Jr., killed by the lover of his mistress, Josie Mansfield.

Vanderbilt and Gould continued to prosper and make even more money. But eventually Daniel Drew lost all his money in a stock market crash and died as he began life, a poor man. Fisk's life also ended tragically. His mistress, Josie Mansfield, betrayed him with Ed Stokes, a handsome and notorious playboy. The two decided to blackmail Fisk with letters he had written Josie that contained embarrassing details of some of his business transactions. At first Fisk paid, for not only did he want to keep his business dealings secret, he also did not want to appear in public as a fool who had been betrayed. But despite the fact that he paid for the letters a number of times, they were never returned as promised. Fisk decided to stop paying, and Josie Mansfield then sued Fisk for the money she claimed he had promised her. Fisk was heartbroken. The press had a field day with the story, and Jay Gould, afraid what the negative publicity might do to the Erie, had Fisk removed from the board of directors. After the first day of the trial, when Jim Fisk dejectedly returned to his hotel, he found Ed Stokes waiting for him with a pistol in his hand. Infuriated by the bad publicity, Stokes fired two bullets into Fisk, killing him. Thus ended the career of perhaps the most colorful of all the robber barons.

Stokes was found guilty of murder and sentenced to hang. However, the appellate court overturned the decision; after two trials, he received a six-year sentence for manslaughter, and served four years in prison.

In the midst of all this manipulation, fraud, and deception, there were a few men of principle who were genuinely interested in building an honest railroad for the good of the people. One was a man by the name of John Poor. In the early 1850s, Poor lived in Portland, Maine, then a small town surrounded by wilderness. Poor saw that Maine would prosper if a railroad connected it with Montreal, Canada. Poor was a very considerate and honest man. Before he drew up plans for a railroad, he visited the people in the most remote forest areas and told them of his plans and asked them how they thought a railroad might help them. He incorporated their answers into his overall plan and presented it to a group of Montreal lawmakers and businessmen. They liked his ideas and agreed to support his railroad. Poor then returned to Portland to draw up the final plans for approval and raise funds for the job. Unknown to him, however, a group of financiers in Boston had learned of his idea and traveled to Montreal to convince the legislators that it would be better for them if the railroad ran from Montreal to Boston rather than Montreal to Portland. They were very convincing and seemed to have persuaded the Canadians. Poor heard of this a week before the final decision was to be made in Montreal. In order to save his railroad, he decided to travel there immediately to convince the legislators not to change their minds. But on the day that he was to leave, there was a terrible blizzard. Everyone warned Poor not to go, but he felt he had no choice. He managed to find a friend willing to accompany him, and the two of them, bundled in furs and blankets, set off together in a horse-drawn carriage into the teeth of the howling storm.

At first they kept to the road, but the snow quickly covered the ground and soon there was no longer any road to be followed. The horses kept drifting into fences and stone walls, or plunging into drifts. The snow beat down so fast and furious that Poor's face was covered with ice. In order to see, he had to clear a little tunnel through the ice that covered his eyes.

Their first destination was a tavern seven miles away. After six hours of stumbling through the storm and almost losing the horses several times, they arrived more dead than alive. Both men and horses were bleeding after being cut by the driving snow. After a good night's sleep, they continued on the next day. Fortunately, a group of men volunteered to clean a path for the horses to pass. The snow was so thick, Poor was only able to average two miles an hour. By nightfall, his nose and ears were frostbitten. Yet, despite the hardship, the worst was yet to come. Poor still had to travel through a pass in the White Mountains of New Hampshire called the Dixville Notch, where the temperatures dropped to eighteen below zero and the winds rushed through at gale force. Poor and his companion pushed on. They inched their way through the notch, the wind whipping the snow around them every step of the way. Finally they made it through the pass and continued until they reached the St. Lawrence River. Although the river was frozen, they managed to find a boatman crazy enough to ferry them across, and Poor arrived at Montreal exactly one hour before the meeting was to take place. His entrance astonished everyone. He eloquently pleaded the case for his railroad and convinced the board. Perhaps they were convinced as much by his courage in making the journey as by his plans. The Portland–Montreal Railroad eventually became a reality. But Poor became deathly ill for almost a year as a result of the journey, which no doubt shortened his life.

By the eve of the Civil War, the railroad builders, great and small, honest and corrupt, ruthless and humanitarian, had covered much of the Northeast and part of the South with railroad tracks. They were about to reach the eastern shores of the river the Indians called "The Father of Waters," the Mississippi, and now, like runners in a race, they were poised and ready to win the greatest and most glorious prize of all—the right to build a railroad that would link the country from the Atlantic to the Pacific. All that was needed to build such a railroad was to cross burning deserts where temperatures sometimes reached 125 degrees in the shade, climb over mountain peaks where the temperature dropped to fifty degrees below zero and the snow was sometimes two hundred feet deep, and pass through Indian and outlaw territory where a railroad worker had to carry a gun along with his pick and shovel. It was a job requiring great courage and imagination, as well as great ruthlessness and deceit. The men who attempted this feat were equal to the task.

Stagecoach in a western city around 1850, of the kind that Mark Twain may have ridden.

3
The Gold Stampede
to California

"I alone of all those afflicted survived"

Gold! The very word fired the imaginations of thousands of people all over the world and inspired them to leave their homes and try to strike it rich in California in 1848.

Because there were no railroads in the West, reaching California overland required traveling by stagecoach or covered wagon across deserts, mountains, and hostile Indian territory. Stagecoach passengers started their trip in Missouri, which was fairly easy to reach by a combination of stagecoach and steamboat. The overland stage from Missouri to San Francisco took seventeen days. One who made the journey was Mark Twain. Riding the stagecoach was an adventure that he described in his book *Roughing It:*

> Our coach was a great swinging and swaying stage . . . an imposing cradle on wheels. It was drawn by six handsome horses and by the side of the driver sat the conductor, the captain of the craft; it was his business to take care of the mails, baggage and passengers. We sat on the back seat

inside. . . . We changed horses every ten miles, all day long and fairly flew over level road. . . . The stage whirled along at a spanking gait, the breeze flapping curtains in a most exhilarating way; the cradle swayed and swung luxuriously; the pattering of the horses' hoofs, the cracking of the driver's whip and his "Hi'yi, glang" were music; the spinning around and the waltzing trees seemed to give us a mute hurrah as we went by . . . and we lay and smoked the pipe of peace and compared all this luxury with the tiresome city life that had gone before it, we felt that there was only one complete and satisfying happiness in the world and we had found it.

But stagecoach travel had its rougher moments as well:

Every time we flew down one bank and scrambled up the other, our party inside got mixed somewhat. First we would all be down in a pile at the forward end of the stage, nearly in a sitting posture, and in a second, we would shoot to the other end and stand on our heads. And we would sprawl and kick to . . . and the majority of us would grumble and say some hasty thing like: "Take your elbow out of my ribs! . . . Quit crowding!"

The hardest part of the trip to San Francisco was crossing the desert. While a stagecoach could usually make eight miles an hour over normal terrain, it was reduced to creeping along at two and a half miles an hour in the desert. Mark Twain looked forward to his first crossing of the desert as a romantic adventure. He was quick to change his mind.

Imagine a vast, waveless ocean stricken dead and turned to ashes; . . . imagine the lifeless silence and solitude that belong to such a place; imagine a coach creeping like a bug through the midst of this shoreless level; . . . imagine this aching monotony kept up hour after hour. . . .

Mark Twain crossed the desert during the day, the worst time of all to pass through that forsaken region:

The sun beats down with dead, blistering relentless malignity; the perspiration is welling from every pore of beast and man; . . . there is not the faintest breath of air stirring; there is not a living creature visible in any direction; there is not a sound—not a sigh—not a whisper—not a buzz or even the whir of wings, or distant bird—not even a sob from the lost souls that doubtless people the dead air.

The alkali dust cut through our lips, it persecuted our eyes, it ate through our delicate membranes and made our noses bleed and kept them bleeding—and truly and seriously, the romance all faded away and disappeared and left the desert trip nothing but a harsh reality—a thirsty sweltering longing, hateful reality.

Among the hardships of the trip that Mark Twain described were the dangers of ambush by Indians and outlaws, sudden torrential rainstorms, cold nights on the prairie, and inedible food and undrinkable coffee. Twelve years later, people would travel from Omaha to Fort Kearny, Nebraska—a trip that took Mark Twain fifty-six hours—in far less time and in far greater luxury. *The New York Times* reported the rail journey as follows:

Upon tables covered with snowy linen and garnished with services of solid silver, . . . waiters flitting about in spotless white placed, as by magic, a repast at which Delmonico [a famous restaurant owner] himself could have had no occasion to blush. . . . After dinner we repaired to our drawing room car and as it was the Sabbath, intoned some grand old hymns. . . . Then to bed in luxurious coaches . . . and only awoke the next morning to find ourselves at the crossing of the North Platte, three hundred miles from Omaha—*fifteen hours and forty minutes out.*

Another way a selected few traveled across country before the railroads was by pony express. The pony express rider had but one job—to deliver the mail from St. Joseph, Missouri, to Sacramento, California, a distance of 1,900 miles, in eight days. Each pony express rider traveled 250 miles in a twenty-four-hour day, twice as much as a stagecoach. There were about eighty riders in the saddle at one time, night and day, between Missouri and California, forty headed east and forty headed west.

The stagecoach carried passengers and limited freight. The pony express carried only mail. For those who wanted to send large amounts of merchandise or who did not want to suffer the hardships of cross-country travel, there was another alternative: ships. Ocean-going vessels carried large amounts of freight and passengers and could be a pleasant way to travel as long as no one was in a hurry and the weather was mild.

To travel from New York to San Francisco by water meant taking a steamer or a sailing boat south past the eastern coasts of the United States and South America, swinging around the stormy Cape

Horn at the tip of South America, and then heading north up the western side of both continents to San Francisco. The distance was 19,000 miles and the trip could take as long as six to seven months. Nor was it always easy. Passengers often had to put up with seasickness, terrible storms, bad food, a tyrannical captain, and boredom. They played cards, checkers, chess, and backgammon; read; attended lectures and poetry readings; sang songs; played practical jokes on each other; and drank as much liquor as they could hold. Their main dish was lobscouse, a hash of potatoes, pork, and hard bread. They often found bugs in the beans, worms in the cereals, and weevils in the flour.

Occasionally a ship sank at sea. In 1853, the ship *Independence* crashed into rocks because of the captain's stupidity. When the passengers warned him that the ship was headed toward the rocks, he insisted that what they saw was only a school of whales, and he refused to change course. The whales, of course, turned out to be rocks. Ezra Down, one of the survivors, described one of the many terrifying moments of that tragedy:

> Men of wealth were offering huge fortunes to be saved. . . .
> Women could be seen climbing down the side of the ship,
> clinging with death-like tenacity to the ropes. Some were
> hanging by their skirts which, in their efforts to jump
> overboard, were caught. As they swung, they were crying
> piteously and horribly, until flames relieved them from this
> awful position, causing them to drop into the ocean and
> sink.

Out of three hundred passengers and crew, 125 drowned.

A Currier and Ives painting of a shipwreck in the mid-nineteenth century,

illustrating the danger of ocean travel.

There was an alternative route. Travelers could take a boat to the Atlantic side of Panama and then cross the isthmus to Panama City on the Pacific side, where they waited for a boat to take them to California. But crossing the isthmus, a distance of only twenty miles, meant traveling through a steaming jungle filled with snakes, tarantulas, and scorpions. It rained every day from May to December. From January to May, the heat never let up. But the worst part of the trip was the boredom of waiting for the passenger ship to San Francisco to arrive and the anxiety of not knowing whether space might be available.

One man who made this journey was Collis P. Huntington, a dry-goods merchant from Connecticut, who was to eventually play a major role in the construction of the first transcontinental railroad. In 1849, after learning that gold had been discovered in California, Huntington decided to leave his prosperous business in the East in the hands of his brother and seek his fortune in the West by selling supplies to those who were seeking gold.

Huntington took the steamer to Panama with a load of merchandise to sell in California. The ship left him and his fellow passengers off at a miserable village at the mouth of the Changres River on the Atlantic coast. From there they traveled westward through the jungle for almost a week, first by boat, then by mule. The heat was unbearable. The mosquitoes were worse. It was not known then that mosquitoes carried malaria and yellow fever, diseases that killed many who caught them. A man by the name of Frank Manyut kept a journal of the trip:

> Our party . . . was half-dead from fatigue, draggled with mud and shivering in torn clothes that for nearly sixty hours had been drenched with rain. The other male passen-

gers—all who had been in good health—made themselves comfortable. . . . In less than ten days, all were dead of yellow fever but one. I alone of all those afflicted survived.

As difficult as the trip across the isthmus was, Panama City on the Pacific coast was even worse. People were sprawled out everywhere, living in the most primitive makeshift huts and tents as they waited for the next boat to San Francisco to arrive. People came down with dysentery from eating unclean fruit, cholera from the primitive sanitation, and malaria from being bitten by mosquitoes. People died from fever every day. Some went mad from boredom. Gambling and drinking, the main occupations, led to fights and killings. Huntington remained aloof from all this, camping in the open, standing guard over his merchandise, and even taking advantage of the situation by peddling native hats, mats, blankets, and patent medicines. Every day, more people would arrive in the crowded colony. It was obvious that there would not be enough boats to take all the waiting people to California. When ships finally arrived, the ship captains sold places to the highest bidder. Many people couldn't afford to pay the exorbitant price, and some of them died of fever before they could find a boat to take them to San Francisco. A few committed suicide; others tried to make the trip in rowboats and were lost at sea. Huntington was one of those who were able to bribe their way on board. The brutal experience of the trip taught him the need for a railroad between California and the East. But before he could play his destined major role in its construction, other events were taking place in the East that would make it possible for him to do so.

The country was not ready yet for a railroad to California. In the year when Collis Huntington journeyed to California, there was not even one railroad line west of the Mississippi River. Nor were the railroad lines east of the Mississippi connected to each other very well, except in the northeast section of the country. In 1849, when a young Illinois lawyer named Abraham Lincoln boarded a train in Washington, D.C., to return to his home in Springfield, Illinois, he had first to ride to a station outside Baltimore, some forty miles away. There he had to change trains for Cumberland, Maryland, 178 miles west of Baltimore, an eleven-hour trip. At Cumberland, Lincoln switched to a stagecoach, which took him 130 miles to Wheeling, Virginia (later West Virginia) in twenty-four hours. At Wheeling, he boarded a steamboat, which traveled down the Ohio River to the Mississippi and then sailed up the Mississippi to St. Louis, Missouri. The steamboat journey took between three and four days. From St. Louis, Lincoln took a stagecoach to Illinois, and when he reached Springfield, he most likely rode to his home on horseback or in a small horse-drawn carriage. The whole trip took him ten days, covered 1,500 miles, and required almost every form of transportation available at the time. (Ten years later, when Lincoln was the sixteenth President of the United States, he could make the same trip entirely by railroad in two days, and travel five hundred fewer miles.)

But all of this was changing. Railroads

Abraham Lincoln at the time he was a trial lawyer for the railroad.

were not only becoming connected, they were moving westward rapidly. On February 22, 1854, thousands of excited spectators gathered on the banks of the Mississippi to watch the first train travel across a railroad bridge spanning the river. For most people, it was a great event, symbolizing the opening of the West to settlers. But not all who watched from the shore were overjoyed. In fact, some were rather sullen and hostile, because for them the success of the railroad meant the end of their way of life. These men owned or worked on the steamboats that carried cargo across the river, and each of them knew that if the railroad succeeded, they would soon be out of work. Some of them decided to resist the building of railroads across the Mississippi. Four months after the bridge's opening, the steamer *Effie Afton* sailed down the Mississippi and crashed into it. The boat caught fire when its stoves overturned, and within minutes both the boat and bridge were in flames.

The steamboat owners were jubilant. They hung up banners that proclaimed: MISSISSIPPI BRIDGE DESTROYED. LET ALL REJOICE. The owners of the boat sued the railroad for damages. They claimed that the bridge made navigation of the river impossible and that all bridges should be banned from crossing the Mississippi. The railroad hired Abraham Lincoln, then one of the top railroad lawyers in the Midwest, to defend it. Before the trial began, Lincoln studied the river in great detail. Gathering masses of information, he showed the jury that given the currents of the river, the depth of the water, and the span of the bridge, the collision couldn't have been an accident. It had to be a deliberate act of sabotage. But most important, Lincoln argued, it was foolish to try to stop bridges from being built across any river. "Rivers were to be crossed," he argued, "and it was the destiny of the American people to move westward." Eventually Lincoln won his case.

The Iron Horse

Lincoln was right. The country was headed westward and it was going by train. Increasing numbers of railroad men and politicians realized that the great American West would remain a wilderness until it was tamed by the railroads. They wanted a railroad that would stretch from Missouri to California. And they didn't recognize or care that by taming the wilderness they would also destroy it.

One visionary was an engineer from Connecticut, Theodore Judah, who in the 1850s dreamed of building a transcontinental railroad that would start in the West, at Sacramento, California, and head east. Before he could accomplish this, Judah first had to figure out a way to cross the Sierra Nevada mountain range in California. The core of the Sierra mountains was solid granite, so hard it could not be dented with a pick and shovel or blasted with dynamite. Even if Judah managed to break down the rock, he would still have to cross a mountain range whose lowest summit was 7,000 feet high and which, in the winter, would be covered by as much as two hundred feet of snow. And the Sierras were not one range, but two!

People predicted that for Judah to build a railroad across the Sierras would require a miracle greater than that of Moses parting the Red Sea. And if by chance this miracle should happen, Judah would still have to cross the deserts of Nevada and Utah, a land filled with poisonous snakes and insects, without water to drink or trees to build fires. And if these obstacles were overcome, the railroad would still have to pass through land inhabited by Native Americans who might object to its being built across their land without their permission. No wonder men called Theodore Judah "crazy."

Yet many people knew that Judah was right in theory, if not in his choice of route. In fact, the federal government made three studies to survey possible routes, one through the north of the country, another through the center, and a third through the south. But the results were undermined by politics. Slavery was a burning issue in America, and there was fierce struggle between Northern and Southern congressmen over whether California would be admitted to the Union as a slave or free state. Both the North and South feared that whichever side got the route for the railroad would win the struggle. As a result, the issue was buried until after Lincoln became president.

As far as Collis Huntington was concerned, there was nothing crazy about Theodore Judah. No doubt he remembered his agonizing trip across Panama ten years earlier. Huntington listened closely to what Theodore Judah had to say about a railroad across the Sierras, and he liked what he heard. He knew that he could make millions if he could build a railroad that would link the West with the East and save people from traveling across seas and jungles or overland by stagecoach. He also saw that a transcontinental railroad could be an essential link in the growing trade between North America, Europe, and Asia.

In 1861 Huntington and three other men formed a railroad company, the Central Pacific, and gave Judah $7,000 to carry out a survey for a railway line. Huntington's associates, who were later called the Big Four, were Mark Hopkins, his partner in the hardware business; Charley Crocker, a dry-goods merchant; and Leland Stanford, a wholesale grocer who was governor of California from 1861 to 1863.

To realize Judah's dream of a transcontinental railroad was a task that would require enormous energy, skill, courage, deceit, and ruthlessness. Collis Huntington and his associates would prove ready and able. But just as they began their venture, the long-simmering hostilities between the North and South finally erupted into civil war. Railroads would play a key role in determining the outcome of the bitter and bloody conflict that followed.

Northern army mortar gun mounted on railway flatcar.

4
The Railroad
Goes to War

*"The object is to move
large masses of men without
the knowledge or consent of anyone"*

As the railroad was connecting the country from one end to the other, slavery was tearing it apart. For almost forty years, a bitter division between North and South was growing over the issue of slavery. Most Northerners wanted to confine slavery to the South and prevent it from spreading to the new states that were joining the Union. Southerners wanted the states to decide for themselves whether they should be slave or free. The South felt that if slavery was prohibited in the new states, then eventually it would be prohibited in the South. In 1860, this conflict exploded into a great civil war.

It was during the Civil War that railroads brought about profound changes in the nature of warfare. Trains became essential for victory on the battlefield. Whichever side transported troops and supplies faster to the right place at the right time would win the war.

The North had the advantage. By 1860, it had 25,000 miles of track, compared to only 10,000 in the South. Equally important, all locomotives in America were built in the North. The Confederacy—the South—lacked factories to construct railroad equipment and was forced to seek help in England. But locomotives took time to build and to ship across the Atlantic Ocean. Moreover, Southern ports were blockaded by Northern ships. As a result, the South had to rely mostly on its prewar equipment and on whatever it could capture from the North.

Another problem that affected the South was the lack of connections between different lines. Materials and troops often had to be taken off one train, transferred to wagons or boats, and transported to the next railway.

During the early years of the conflict, many of the railroad's problems were caused by the ignorance of soldiers rather than by the war itself. Many were slow to grasp the military significance of trains. Officers treated railroads as a means of transportation for their own convenience, as if they were passenger lines. One general who was traveling with his wife in a railway car decided to stop the train on the tracks so that his wife could rest overnight in a farmhouse. By doing so, he held up the whole line, and neither troops nor supplies could be moved until the general and his wife started out again the next day.

Lincoln's secretary of war, Edwin Stanton, realizing he had to solve this problem immediately, chose two men to run the railroad. They were Colonel Daniel C. McCallum, whom Stanton appointed military director and supervisor of the railroads, and Colonel Herman Haupt, a man who hated to wear uniforms and refused to take any pay for his services. McCallum's job was to plan and supervise the overall strategy for the Union railroad. Haupt was the man in the field to keep the trains moving. Between the two of them, they made the Northern railroads among the most effective fighting elements of the war.

Although the two men were only colonels, they were given full authority over the railroad. No one was allowed to interfere with the running of the trains. Congress backed up this position by authorizing the U.S. government to take over the railroads in 1862.

This new law was put to the test when General Carl Schurz, a prominent New York politician commissioned as a general, became separated from his troops. He ordered Colonel Haupt to stop all trains and send him on a special train to catch up. Haupt refused. Furious, General Schurz wired Secretary Stanton, telling him that a colonel had dared to countermand the order of a general and should be court-martialed and discharged. Stanton wired back and told Schurz to shut up and stop interfering with the railroad or else he would discharge *him*.

The South also had its share of problems. The main difficulty was that the Confederacy lacked a strong central authority to regulate the railroads and coordinate movements. Many lines remained in private hands or were under control of the governors of the individual states. The owners firmly believed that the railroads' stockholders were entitled to make a fair profit, war or no war. Also, passenger travel was sometimes given precedence over military needs. In Georgia the state owned and operated the railroads during the war and the governor treated them as his private lines. He decided that the Confederate army should pay double what it cost to transport civilians and freight. When one general threatened to seize the line, the governor threatened to shut it down completely. The general backed off, but not without a few curses under his breath.

The Confederate army was often shortsighted. Like their Northern counterparts, Southern officers tended to use trains for their own personal convenience. Sometimes when they received boxcars filled with supplies, they kept the cars to use as warehouses rather than unloading and returning them. As a result, the South lost the use of many cars. Practices like these forced soldiers to "borrow" trains and even rails and ties from other lines, usually without returning them.

Sometimes an officer would take it upon himself to send or hold a train. In Virginia, an officer, not wanting to divide his troops, refused to transport desperately needed reinforcements to a battlefield until he could send them all together. As empty trains arrived to rush soldiers to the fighting, he held them up until he had enough boxcars to transport all the troops at once. By that time it was too late and the battle was lost. In another case, as troops and civilians in Atlanta, Georgia, were fleeing from the advancing Northern army, an officer requisitioned a passenger train and put the wounded on board. Unfortunately, he failed to notify the railroad what he was doing. The tragic result was a head-on collision with another train outside of Atlanta. Thirty men died, two locomotives were lost, and the line was tied up for hours, preventing it from being used to help others escape.

Despite the many obstacles and mistakes, both sides were able to put railroads to good use. The first major battle in which the railroad made a difference between victory and defeat was the battle of Bull Run—the first battle of the Civil War. The Union soldiers were undisciplined and naive, and thought they could whip the rebels easily. They treated the battle more as a game than as a matter of life and death. Each regiment of soldiers had its own fancy outfit, as if it were going on a parade rather than fighting a war. Congressmen came to watch the battle from a nearby hill as if it were a sporting event. Senators brought their wives and children, who packed picnic baskets in case they got hungry while the fighting was going on. Then comedy became tragedy. The Confederates, although outnumbered at first, were grim and determined. They blasted the Northern troops with cannons and rifles, and soon men and horses were lying on the ground torn and bleeding. Yet the Union armies held their ground and might have won, when suddenly Confederate trains began to arrive, carrying fresh troops into the fighting. One after another the trains unloaded soldiers, who rushed into battle. Their arrival turned the battle in the South's favor. The Union troops panicked and ran all the way back to Washington, with the congressional picnickers fleeing ahead of them.

One of the North's most effective uses of a railroad came during the battle of Gettysburg. During the battle, Colonel Haupt sent cars filled with supplies to the battlefield and then loaded the empty cars with wounded soldiers and brought them to hospitals on the return trip. Haupt moved 1,500 tons of supplies to the front lines daily and carried out thousands of wounded soldiers. The trains used specially designed, highly comfortable hospital cars to transport the wounded. By comparison, the South lacked a railroad at Gettysburg and was forced to transport its wounded by wagon. The bumpy, rough ride was often more agonizing to the soldiers than the wounds themselves. Many Southern soldiers died who might have been saved had they been transported by train.

Since railroads were the key to victory, both North and South desperately tried to destroy each other's lines. The South was usually more effective, as bands of Southern soldiers carried out constant hit-and-run attacks. In one spectacular raid in 1861, a group of Confederate soldiers attacked the Baltimore and Ohio Railroad yards in Martinsburg, Virginia. They destroyed fifty-six locomotives and three hundred cars and were even able to dismantle several locomotives and carry them back to the South on wagons. It was one of the worst attacks on Northern railroads during the war.

One of the most heroic and tragic railroad attacks took place in 1862, when a group of Union soldiers led by James Andrews tried to

Northern army train derailed by Confederate guerrillas.

steal a Confederate train in Georgia and take it across to Union lines in Tennessee. The plan was part of a harebrained scheme by a Union general to destroy one of the South's railroads. It was never clear what difference it would have made if Andrews stole the locomotive, but he was a brave if not bright man and was willing to do what he was asked.

Andrews and his men dressed in civilian clothes and slipped behind Southern lines. They then boarded a Southern train in Alabama, pretending they were recruits on their way to join the Confederate army in Virginia. When the train stopped for a meal break in Georgia, Andrews and his men unhitched the locomotive and three cars and took off for the North. The Confederate captain of the train, W. A. Fuller, immediately began to chase them. He and his men started off in a flatcar. When that proved useless, they switched to an old locomotive. Andrews, despite his head start, was constantly being delayed. He had made the mistake of traveling on a Monday, when the line was filled with other trains, instead of on a Sunday, when the line would have been empty. As a result, he was forced to stop and wait several times until other trains were moved out of the way onto side tracks so he could pass.

Whenever he was questioned about where he was going, Andrews said that he was carrying gunpowder to the front lines of the Confederate army. To prevent his pursuers from catching him, Andrews burned bridges and tried to destroy the tracks behind him. He also destroyed telegraph lines as he traveled, so that his pursuers could not wire ahead to have him stopped. But no matter what obstacles Andrews created, Fuller managed to overcome them. Finally Andrews's train began to run out of steam, long before he reached the Union lines. He and his men abandoned the train and ran into the woods. They were eventually tracked down by Confederate soldiers.

The funeral car of Abraham Lincoln, which was designed and built by George Pullman.

One of the rules of war was that any soldier caught in civilian clothes was considered a spy, which meant death by hanging. The Southerners showed no mercy. Eight of the men captured were hanged, including Andrews.

Gradually, as the North gained the upper hand in the fighting, it launched an all-out attack on Southern railroads. When General Sherman began his famous march through Georgia, he laid waste to hundreds of miles of railroad tracks, forcing the Southern army to retreat. At the same time Sherman was destroying enemy railroads, he was receiving a steady stream of supplies from his own railroad in the early stages of his campaign.

The most famous train ride related to the Civil War was also the saddest: A train carried the body of President Abraham Lincoln from Washington, D.C., to Springfield, Illinois, after his assassination by John Wilkes Booth, on April 15, 1865, at the war's end.

On April 21, Lincoln's body was placed on a special train. Black soldiers lined the station as an honor guard. Slowly the train left Washington for its sad 1,700-mile voyage, its locomotive draped in black crepe, flying American flags, and displaying a picture of the president. In every city and town it passed, thousands upon thousands of mourning Americans, tears streaming down their faces, paid tribute. The train stopped in major cities so that people could pay their last respects. In Albany, four thousand people an hour filed by the coffin. Bonfires lighted its way at night and cannons sounded its arrival during the day. When the train arrived in Chicago, the president's coffin was transferred to the most luxurious sleeping car in America, the Pioneer, designed by a young inventor by the name of George Pullman. It was used to transport the president's body to Springfield. No matter how small the town, the train slowed down and tolled its bell until it reached Springfield, where the president was finally laid to rest.

The transcontinental railroad—a lifeline connecting landlocked towns and industries to the port cities of the East and West. (Currier & Ives lithograph, 1870, The New York Public Library)

5
The Railroad
Unites America

*"Work as though heaven
were before you
and hell behind"*

The Civil War had divided America. The transcontinental railroad would help unite it. But both Collis Huntington and Theodore Judah saw the war as an opportunity to get the backing they needed to build their transcontinental railroad. As men clashed and died on battlefields to determine whether the country would be slave or free, the two tycoons struggled with Congress to determine which of them would become the richest man in America.

The Civil War proved to be a blessing in disguise for Judah and Huntington. It made Congress aware of how important a transcontinental railroad was to the country. Both men played upon the fact that California and Nevada, with their great wealth in silver and gold, were highly vulnerable to attack by the South as long as these states were not linked by rail with the North. They argued that only a railroad would allow the army to send troops to protect the mines there. One of the strong supporters of the transcontinental railroad was President Abraham Lincoln, who, as a lawyer for the railroad, had successfully defended the building of bridges across the Mississippi years earlier.

The key to building the railroad was held by Congress. Huge amounts of land and money were needed for the task, and only Congress could supply both. It had already given several million acres of land to smaller railroad lines. To build a transcontinental road would require grants of over 21 million square acres of land and $50 million in loans. The railroads could use the land as collateral to borrow money.

In 1862, Lincoln signed a bill that gave Huntington and Judah the land grants and loans the Central Pacific needed to build a transcontinental railroad. It would begin in Sacramento, California, and head east to Utah, where it would join with another railroad, the Union Pacific. Congress granted the Central Pacific nine million acres of land and lent it $24 million, a sum determined by the number of miles of track the railroad would have to build. For every mile in flat country, the government would lend the Central Pacific $16,000; for every mile of track laid in the foothills to the mountains, it would lend $32,000; and for every mile of track in the mountains, $48,000. When the legislation was passed, Judah cabled back to California, "We have drawn the elephant. Now let us see if we can harness him."

But Congress was not going to allow the Big Four to be the only ones to build a transcontinental railroad. The same bill that gave the Central Pacific the authority to construct a line that ran west to east also commissioned another railroad company, the Union Pacific, to build a line east to west, starting at Council Bluffs, Missouri. The land grant was twelve million acres and the loan was $27 million. It may also have helped that certain key congressmen and senators received stocks in the railroads at low rates from both railroads.

The plan was for the two railroads to meet somewhere in Utah, the exact place to be specified later. The Union Pacific would lay approximately a thousand miles of track and the Central Pacific seven hundred. However, the Central Pacific had the hardest part of the job. It had to cross the Sierra Nevada mountains and the Nevada desert before it reached its goal.

Both railroads were motivated by the same factor: profit. The more track they could construct, the more money they would make. And so it became a race between the two lines to see which could lay down the most track. Millions of dollars were at stake. Many short-cuts would be taken: Bridges would be poorly constructed and roads improperly graded. Eventually much of the work had to be redone. But despite all the corruption, inefficiency, and inferior work, the building of the transcontinental railroad was one of the marvels of the nineteenth century.

The Union Pacific was controlled by Thomas Durant, a man of considerable energy and charm with a dark reputation as a wheeler-dealer and manipulator. Durant was a shady character, a lone wolf, whose every business venture was a scheme of some sort. His plan was to organize a construction company that would be awarded all contracts to build the Union Pacific. Called the Crédit Mobilier, the company issued bonds that Durant passed out as bribes to congress-men. Crédit Mobilier was responsible for the construction of the railroad and overcharged it for everything. Thus, if a barrel of nuts and bolts normally cost $25, Durant would charge the Union Pacific $50 and put the profit in his own pocket or in the pockets of his friends. It was robbery, but there was no law against it. The construc-tion company made huge profits, while the railroad eventually went bankrupt.

If the completion of the railroad were up to Durant alone, it might have gone bankrupt before it was built. Fortunately, Durant hired

General Grenville Dodge, a Civil War hero, as the chief engineer for the project. Durant couldn't have made a better choice. Whereas he was interested in using the railroad to enrich himself, Dodge was interested in seeing the railroad built. He was honest, fearless, and extremely competent, and he refused to go along with many of Durant's schemes. They often clashed head-on, and Dodge usually won.

But if Dodge was a match for Thomas Durant, Theodore Judah was no match for the Big Four. Judah's problem was that he was stubborn and relatively honest. He did not like or trust his partners very much, nor they him. It was inevitable that a conflict would break out. When Charley Crocker, one of the partners, set up a construction company to sell supplies to the railroad at the highest possible price (as Durant was doing), Judah protested. He forced Crocker to drastically scale down his prices, at least temporarily. The partners also tried to change the survey map so that it would appear that the foothills began where there was actually flatland. Since the rate for building in the foothills was $32,000, as opposed to $16,000 in flatland, they stood to make an enormous profit. Judah again protested. This time, Huntington issued an ultimatum: Either Judah must buy them out, or they would buy Judah out. When Judah couldn't come up with the money, Huntington bought his interest for $100,000 in railroad stock. Judah then took ship back to New York to get support in his struggle against his former partners. While crossing Panama, he caught yellow fever and died, no doubt to their relief.

The task of supervising the construction of the Central Pacific Railroad now fell to Charley Crocker, a rough and ready bull of a man, who was stubborn, vain, and determined. The man who replaced Thomas Judah was an engineer by the name of Samuel Montague, who was cut from the same mold as Crocker. Together, they

Crew laying track on the Union Pacific.

had the awesome task of crossing two mountain ranges and a desert to complete their part of the railroad.

In 1863, the great race to build a transcontinental railroad officially began. The construction crews of the Central Pacific laid down the first tracks outside Sacramento, California, to cheers and celebrations, which were pure public relations. Huntington had not yet secured all the money he needed to build his railroad. In the first year, only eighteen miles of track were completed. By the end of 1864, only twelve more miles had been built. In Missouri, the Union Pacific had not even started its part of the line. But as a result of political maneuvers, Collis Huntington persuaded the federal government to come up with the money he needed to continue, and by 1865, the year the Civil War ended, Crocker was ready to roll. He would not stop for another five years and one thousand miles.

At first, the work went smoothly and the crews worked at a rapid pace. There was rhythm and order to the construction. First the graders leveled the earth; then the tiemen laid down the ties. They were followed by the ironmen, who set the track in place; each rail weighed between 560 and 700 pounds. The ironmen were followed by the spikemen, who secured the rails to the ties. Last came the track liners, who aligned the track and made sure it was straight.

As the track approached the Sierra mountains, Crocker noticed that many of his workers began to quit. He soon discovered that the only reason they had signed up to work on the railroad was to get close to the silver mines of Nevada. Desperately short of labor, Crocker feared that he might not have enough men to complete his railroad. One of his partners, Leland Stanford, then governor of California, made a suggestion. Why not try Chinese laborers?

Crocker thought it was a great idea. Ever since gold had been discovered in California, the Chinese had been immigrating to the

This photograph shows an example of how difficult it was to grade the transcontinental railroad. This site was four miles west of Omaha, Nebraska. The land was first cut into shelves and then each shelf was leveled by dynamite and pickaxes until the grade was even.

United States in hopes of becoming rich. In 1850, 4,000 had arrived. The following year, 25,000 came. By 1860, there were 35,000 Chinese, over half of whom worked in the gold fields. Most of them had come from the Sze-yap region in China's Kwangtung province, where a violent civil war was raging between different Chinese ethnic groups. Life was very hard there and the average income was between $3 and $5 a month. When news came that gold had been discovered in California, thousands of young men tried to immigrate. A letter from a Chinese man living in Boston to his family told of the great wealth thought to be found there: "Good Americans speak of California. Oh, very rich country. They find gold very quickly I hear. Every day, two three pounds of gold."

The Chinese called California Kum-Shan, the "Gold Mountain." Thousands sought passsage there. The fare was about $50, which was too expensive for most people. Many families would pool their resources to send one member over. Others would take out a mortgage on their land; some men put their wife and children up for pledges. This practice got to be so bad that one moneylender advertised:

> Labor wanted in the land of the USA. There are many good works. They will provide good house and plenty of food. They will pay you $28 a month. There is no fear of slavery. The ship is now going and will take all who can pay passage. The money required is $54. Persons having property may have it sold. *I cannot take security on your wife and child.*

Interest rates were high. To borrow $50 often meant that the borrower had to pay back at least $100 and often more, depending on how long he took to repay the loan.

The crossing took two to three months and the ships were usually overcrowded and filthy. Ten percent of the immigrants died on the voyage. Most of those who made the journey were young, unmarried men.

As soon as they landed in California, the Chinese were ready to go to work. In order to pay back their loans, many started working the day they arrived. They were willing to take any job at any price. In the cities and towns, many worked as laundrymen, housemen, and gardeners. They worked long and hard without complaining, earning an average of a dollar a day. Whatever they saved, they sent to their families in China. Many traveled to the gold fields and worked the leftover dirt for the smallest pieces of gold—diggings other miners had left behind.

In California, the Chinese suffered terribly from racism and dis-crimination. They were not allowed to attend public schools, vote, or testify in court against a white person. If a white man murdered a Chinese, he was seldom convicted. As a result, hundreds of Chinese were slaughtered, many by miners who envied their ability to extract gold in places that other miners had long abandoned. Special taxes were levied against them; one tax collector noted in his diary, after killing a Chinese man who had argued about his bill: "I was sorry to stab that fellow but the law makes the tax necessary and that's where I get my profit." Gangs of whites tormented Chinese men by cutting off their hair, which they wore tied behind their backs in a long pigtail called a queue. (The Chinese began wearing queues during the four-teenth century after they were conquered by the Mongols, who wore their hair in that fashion.) The gangs used to compete with one another to see who could collect the largest number of queues and make belts out of them.

Crocker immediately saw the wisdom of hiring the Chinese. They looked small and weak, but they were willing to work longer and harder than anyone else. When Crocker's superintendent asked, "How are those rice-eating weaklings going to build a railroad?" Crocker replied, "They built the Great Wall of China, didn't they? That was almost as tough a job as a railroad."

The first group of fifty Chinese arrived at a railroad camp in the middle of a forest. They ate a meal of dried fish and rice and went to sleep. At dawn, they arose, took up their heavy picks, shovels, and wheelbarrows, put on their basket hats, blue shirts, pantaloons, and slippers, and began to work. Twelve hours later they were still at it. They were so eager for work that they would light huge fires at night in order to continue working after dark.

The Chinese worked out so well that Crocker immediately sent to China for more workers. Advertisements for workers were posted throughout Kwangtung province. They read: "Come over and help us. We have plenty of money to spend but no one to earn it." For their hard work, the Chinese earned $30 a month in gold and silver, out of which they had to pay about $18 for their food and lodging. (By comparison, white workers were paid $60 a month.) Out of this salary, most Chinese sent home an average of $30 a year, about six to ten months' wages in China. The rest they kept for their own expenses.

The Chinese way of life was much different from that of other workers. They ate oysters, raw cuttlefish, rice, and occasionally a little pork, but they avoided beef and potatoes—the main foods of the Irish crews. They had no women. They liked to gamble and smoke opium when not working. They were treated brutally and with contempt, but there is no record of their complaining. The Irish whom Crocker had hired before the Chinese arrived were hostile at first. They contemptuously called the Chinese "Crocker's pets." But when they saw that the Chinese would do all the manual labor and dangerous

Chinese workers clearing away the rubble after blasting. The Chinese made up most of the work force of the crews working eastward from California to Utah.

work and the status jobs would be reserved for them, the Irish reluctantly accepted the Chinese. They even came to admire them for their courage and dedication to hard work.

Most of the Chinese workers did not intend to remain in America. They accepted the fact that they would suffer terribly here. Their dream was to make enough money to have a happy and comfortable old age in China, where they would not have to work and would be respected and admired by their families and friends. One of the most important parts of their agreement with the railroad was that if a Chinese worker died in America, his remains would be shipped back to China so that his bones could be buried among his ancestors. No Chinese immigrant wanted his ghost wandering around in a strange and alien land.

By 1866, there were six thousand Chinese at work on the Central Pacific. Crocker had long passed the California flatlands and foothills and had finally reached the Sierra Nevada. Now came the moment of truth. Could his men lay railroad tracks over one of the roughest mountain ranges in America? Could his crews build a railroad over cliffs thousands of feet high, which were covered with snow at least six months of the year? Crocker said they could, and he swore to do everything in his power to see that they would.

The first assault team was the Chinese workers. They scampered up the mountainside carrying picks and shovels. They clung to the side of granite cliffs while they cut gaps wide enough for a train to pass. They made their way up steep inclines, carrying two seventy-pound bags of blasting powder on their backs, each bag balanced on the end of a pole. When the workers came to a cliff where there was no natural foothold, they had to create one; they were lowered from the top on ropes alongside the cliff, with nothing between them and the ground but several thousand feet of air. They worked suspended in the air twelve hours a day cutting a ledge on the cliff with hammers and chisels. Once they created a path, their fellow workers would widen it and lay track. At times, the workers in baskets would have to blast the rock away. They would chisel a small hole in the rock, fill it with blasting powder, light the fuse, and frantically signal to be pulled up to safety. If the crew pulling the basket up was too slow, the blast would send the men in the basket to their deaths in the gorge thousands of feet below.

In addition to creating ledges and laying tracks on the edges of cliffs, Crocker's men dug fifteen tunnels. At times, the granite was so thick, picks and chisels broke against its surface. In some places, blasting powder turned the rock black but didn't make a dent. Finally, a Swedish chemist by the name of Swansen was called in; he devised a nitroglycerin explosive to do the job. It blasted the rock, but it blasted crews as well. In fact, it was so dangerous that Crocker used it only when absolutely necessary. One tunnel turned out to be the most expensive quarter-mile in railroad history. It cost $5 million to dig. It took thousands of Chinese laborers one full year to cut through a quarter-mile rock. They averaged only eight inches of tunnel a day. A new invention, the steam drill, was available and could have done the job in half the time and at half the cost, but Crocker stubbornly refused to try it without ever fully explaining why.

By May of 1866, ninety-four miles of track had been laid and 15,000 Chinese men were at work. A Sacramento newspaper reporter who visited the camp wrote about them:

> Systematic workers these Chinese, competent and wonder-
> fully effective because tireless and unremitting in their
> energy. They are paid $30–$35 a month out of which they
> board themselves. They . . . save $20 a month. They work

from sunrise to sunset six days a week. They spend Sunday washing and mending, gambling, smoking and frequently . . . quarreling.

From spring to fall, it was a dangerous and difficult job to build a railroad through the mountains. During the winter, it was considered reckless and impossible. Yet Crocker was racing against time, and he could not afford a winter vacation. He pushed his workers on despite the fact that fifteen feet of snow covered the construction line. Inch by inch the Chinese crews had to clear a path so that rails could be laid down. Some men froze to death. Others lost fingers and hands to frostbite. Supplies were transported by dogsled, and when the supply route became impassable, Crocker dug a tunnel and shipped everything underground.

But the worst danger was from avalanches. On a clear, still day a crew might suddenly hear a rumbling noise, like a thunderstorm in the distance. All the men would suddenly stop working and look up in terror to see if an avalanche was sweeping down on them. When that happened, there was nowhere to flee. A river of snow came rushing down the mountainside, burying the crew and carrying them to the bottom of the canyon, where they would remain until the spring, when the snow melted and their bodies could be found.

Yet despite all these obstacles Crocker pushed on. He drove his men to their breaking point, but he asked nothing of anyone he was not willing to do himself. He was the general of an army who stood in the front line of fire, sharing the hardships and danger with his men. And they respected him for it and allowed themselves to be driven forward. Inch by inch, foot by foot, yard by yard, mile by mile, railroad track was laid down across the Sierras.

The Sierra Nevada Mountains of California were a huge obstacle for the Central Pacific crews. Train track through the mountains often followed riverbeds and other natural passes. (Currier & Ives print, 1871, The New York Public Library)

The Iron Horse

As the Central Pacific struggled with the Sierra Nevada, the Union Pacific also had its share of problems. General Dodge had the same problem as the Central Pacific—getting enough men for the job. Many men had joined the army when the Civil War began, causing a shortage of American workers. As Crocker got his Chinese workers almost directly off the boat from China, Dodge also turned to immigrant labor, getting his workers directly from Ireland. Workers arrived on the East Coast and were immediately shipped to the construction site in Missouri. When the Civil War ended, Dodge also picked up a large number of ex-soldiers, many of whom had become drifters and outlaws.

The two men who ran the work crews for the Union Pacific were the Casement brothers—General Jack and his brother, Dan. Dan was only five feet four but a bulldog of a man, as fierce as they come. The only man shorter and fiercer was his brother, Jack, who was described as being "five feet nothing." The two brothers were called "the biggest little men you'll ever see." They were even more determined than General Dodge to see that the railroad was built.

The crews of the Union Pacific had a much easier construction job than the crews of the Central Pacific. The land was relatively flat and there were few mountains to cross. Construction began in the great prairies of the Midwest, and for most of the Irish, the land and its people were a source of wonder and astonishment. The countryside seemed flat and unending. There was not a tree or a shrub anywhere. Farther west, the crews saw the great buffalo herds that inhabited the plain. The herds were so large that when they crossed the railroad tracks they could delay a train for hours. The crews also saw coyotes, antelopes, jackrabbits, prairie dogs, grasshoppers, and rattlesnakes.

The major difficulty Dodge and his men had to face were the Native

Americans. (Collis Huntington solved his problems with them by giving the chiefs free passes to ride on his trains, including the locomotive. The rest of the tribe could ride for free on the freight trains.) The tribes had not been consulted about having a railroad run through what had traditionally been their hunting grounds. They had no objection to people hunting there or passing through. But the railroad was another matter. The Plains Indians—mainly the Sioux, Cheyenne, Kiowa, and Arapaho—saw clearly that the railroad was the death blow to their way of life. Iron Bull, the Crow chief, summed up the significance of the railroad for his people: "We have reached the end of our rule and a new one has come. The end of our lives, too, is near at hand. . . . Of our once powerful nation there are now but a few left . . . and we too, will soon be gone."

The truth was that the railroad developers, like the gold hunters and farmers, wanted the land of the Indian peoples. In order to convince the federal government to send in the army to wipe out the tribes, they argued that the Indians were dangerous and needed to be subdued, if not wiped out. But before they were defeated, the Plains Indians put up a struggle that lasted for almost thirty years. In 1865, Red Cloud, a Sioux chief, warned of what was to come: "You destroyed the buffalo, you lied to us, you will get nothing from us but war." Two hundred miles west of Missouri, the Cheyennes, under Chief Spotted Tail, attacked and plundered a train, killed its crew, and destroyed the track. Raiding parties continually ambushed advance parties of surveyors. In the Black Hills, General Dodge himself was attacked while looking for a route through the mountains for the railroad. He barely escaped.

One of the most famous encounters between the Native Americans and the Union Pacific took place in 1868 at Plum Creek, Nebraska. A group of Sioux warriors waited by a railroad track for a train to come. Years later one of the members of the raiding party told the story:

The Iron Horse

The white soldiers had run us from our lodges and hunting grounds. They burned everything we had. Our blankets were ragged. Our ponies thin. We needed the white man's medicine. We thought if we could take what was inside the iron horse, we could become strong again.

The raiding party ripped up sections of the track to cause a derailment and then waited in ambush for a freight train. But instead, a flatcar appeared, carrying several men who were inspecting the track. The flatcar derailed and the Indians attacked, killing two of the crew and wounding a third, Willie Thompson. Thompson pretended he was dead even as one of the Indians scalped him. Miraculously, he survived. The Sioux then continued to wait for a freight train. When it finally appeared, it crashed into the flatcar and derailed. Thompson watched as the fireman and engineer were killed and the Sioux broke open the freight cars to plunder them. Thompson noticed that the Indian who had taken his scalp dropped it. After the raiders left, he got up, picked up his scalp, and waited until he was rescued. He took his scalp to a doctor, hoping that he might be able to sew it back in place. When the operation was unsuccessful, Thompson donated the scalp to the Omaha, Nebraska, public library, where it was displayed for many years as one of their prime exhibits.

The United States Army, under General William Sherman, was finally sent in to drive the Plains Indians out of the railroad's territory. Sherman's goal was to either make peace with the tribes through treaties or destroy them militarily. More often than not, the treaties were broken by the whites. The army also wiped out a number of peaceful Indian villages, massacring men, women, and children and then reporting the event as a great battle, when in fact there had been no resistance. Colonel George Custer, who would eventually be killed

A group portrait taken in 1870 in Washington of Chief Red Cloud of the
Sioux Indians with other leaders who gathered to sign a peace treaty.

by the Sioux at the battle of the Little Big Horn in 1876, led some of the most notorious massacres. In retaliation, a Cheyenne chief named Tall Bull led his Dog Soldiers, as his warriors were called, against the railroad, wrecking trains and killing their crews. The army tracked them and finally located Tall Bull's camp. They attacked, killing him and most of his followers.

The United States not only destroyed the society and culture of the Plains Indians, it also destroyed their means of survival. The buffalo was the winter source of food for most of the tribe and a major source of clothing to protect people from the bitter winter cold. Buffalo hunters like William "Buffalo Bill" Cody slaughtered buffalo to supply the railroad workers with food, while others massacred the herds just for the "sport." Between 1865 and 1885, some twelve million buffalo were slaughtered by white hunters, soldiers, and railroad passengers.

By 1900 the Indian wars had ended. Out of an estimated one million Native Americans who lived on this continent when the first European settlers arrived in Jamestown, Virginia, three hundred years earlier, only 300,000 were left.

The arrival of the United States Army made the work somewhat safer for the Union Pacific crews. But the railroad had other problems as well, especially with gamblers, whiskey salesmen, and prostitutes who followed the railroad workers, trying to rob them of their money. They set up mobile camps called Hells-on-Wheels, which followed the crews as the work progressed. One man described these traveling sin towns as follows:

> Almost everybody is dirty . . . filthy, marked with the
> lowest vice. There is a murder a day, gambling, drinking

Bear River City, one of the typical Hells-on-Wheels. It had two hundred inhabitants, most of whom were saloonkeepers and prostitutes. When railroad construction moved on, the town closed down and reopened farther along the line.

and the lowest of sexual commerce. Where these people are from, where they went to when the road was finished, were puzzles to me. Hell would appear to have been razed to furnish them. And it is to there they may have eventually returned.

The situation became so bad that Dodge finally telegraphed his supervisors to take care of the "bad men." The Casement brothers gathered the roughest men of his crew, the ironmen, and paid a visit to the gamblers' camp. They politely told the gamblers that they had one hour to pack up and leave or remain where they were until Judgment Day. When General Dodge arrived some weeks later, he asked Jack Casement if the problem had been solved. Dodge was taken to the now deserted gambler's camp and shown the fresh graves in which perhaps as many as thirty of the more prominent "bad men" were now "quietly" resting "with their boots on."

With the army guarding the railroad from Indian attacks and the gambling towns somewhat controlled, the Union Pacific began to move rapidly westward. Since Congress had not set a point at which the Union Pacific was to join with the Central Pacific, both planned to go as far as they could, even if they passed each other. The goal for each was to lay down as much track as possible in order to be paid as much as possible. By 1868, it seemed certain that the Union Pacific would win the race. Winter was coming, and Crocker and his Central Pacific crews would most likely be stuck in the mountains until spring.

Crocker was about to face his last major challenge, a mountain of sheer granite above the Donner Pass. Crocker had built part of the railroad on the western and eastern ends of the pass, but the trick was to join them. He told Huntington that the pass would be buried under fifty feet of snow and work couldn't begin until spring. Huntington was desperate. He couldn't wait until spring. Millions of dollars were at stake. "Close that gap," he ordered Crocker, "if you have to melt the snow in tin cups." Winter set in, but Crocker refused to stop work. He brought in two hundred carpenters and 2,500 skilled workers to cut 65 million board feet of lumber and build snowsheds that covered thirty-seven of the forty miles of that impossible summit crossing. The sheds kept out the snow and the men were able to work on the tracks underneath as if they were in a thirty-seven-mile-long barn. As the work progressed slowly, Huntington telegraphed Crocker: "Work as though heaven was before you and hell behind you." Every mile built in the flatland of the desert yielded 100 percent profit. Aware that the Union Pacific was winning the mileage race, the Central Pacific crews made a superhuman effort, and by spring of 1868 they crossed the Sierras and reached the deserts of Nevada.

Once over the mountains, the work went fast. The railroad passed through an area owned by a man named Lake; Crocker made a deal with him for his land. In turn, the railroad built a town overnight in the desert. It was called Reno, and within months, where before there had been a wasteland, stood a wide-open town complete with saloons, gamblers, prostitutes, fiddlers, speculators, and even a few respectable people.

Meanwhile, the Central Pacific crews in the desert were working in temperatures that reached 120 in the shade. Water had to be brought from forty miles away. The working conditions were so bad that the salaries of the Chinese were raised to $35 a month. What saved them from collapsing in the heat was their broad "coolie" hats, which protected them from the broiling sun. The work animals were not so lucky. One engineer wrote:

> Our livestock was suffering for lack of water. The mules made the night hideous with their frightful cries. One hundred mules uniting their voices in chorus, kicking at

THEY ARE PRETTY SAFE THERE.

"GIVE IT TO HIM, HE'S GOT NO VOTE NOR NO FRIENDS!"

A political cartoon showing the deep prejudice against the Chinese among American whites. The cartoon shows how almost all whites, despite their political differences, agreed on one thing—their hatred of the Chinese.

each other in a vain effort to escape and quench their burning thirst.

As the two crews competed to lay down the most track, the main battle was fought in Washington. Huntington realized that the Union Pacific was laying down more track than his Central Pacific and would receive far greater benefits unless he could stop the Union Pacific politically and financially. Huntington was successful. He was able to get from Congress money due him for completing another phase of the construction earlier than expected. To get this money, part of his line had to pass an inspection by government officials. Technically, the line was incomplete. However, Huntington's men got the inspectors drunk and they certified the line anyway without examining it too closely. More important, Huntington managed to block Durant from getting the funds he needed by having part of the work done by the Union Pacific judged as being outside the contract and ineligible for grants.

Meanwhile, as Huntington was wheeling and dealing in Washington, the crews of both railroads entered Utah from opposite sides and were fast approaching each other. Instead of joining up, however, they passed each other. As the crews from both railroads began to work close to one another, battles broke out. The Union Pacific Irish felt contempt for the Central Pacific Chinese and wasted no time expressing it. The Irish started fights with the Chinese workers and occasionally shot them. The Chinese "accidentally" rolled boulders on the Irish. In retaliation, the Irish laid dynamite charges close to the Chinese, looking innocent when the blasts threw Chinese workers and their horses, wheelbarrows, and tools skyward. The Chinese returned the compliment. A full-scale war might have broken out between the two crews, but Durant and Huntington decided to call a

The joining of the east and west tracks of the transcontinental railroad. The date is May 10, 1869; the place, Promontory Point, Utah. The train on the left is from the Central Pacific. The train on the right is from the Union Pacific. The two rails were joined with a golden spike, which was later removed so that it wouldn't be stolen.

truce and Congress finally set a place where the railroads were to join each other. Before they were officially joined, the railroads held a contest to see whose crews could lay more track in one day. The Union Pacific crew laid down eight miles of track in a single day, which was considered a record. The Central Pacific met the challenge. Beginning at dawn, its crews worked nonstop, without breaking for lunch or asking for relief. When the day was over, the crew had set down ten miles of track. It was a great feat.

Finally, on May 10, 1869, in the little locality of Promontory Point, Utah, which consisted of five saloons, all built just before the celebration, a crowd of some five hundred partially sober people gathered to watch the Union Pacific and the Central Pacific join their tracks. Each railroad had sent a locomotive, so the two engines faced each other at the point where the line was to be joined. Thomas Durant arrived late. He had been held up, literally, by a group of his workers who took him prisoner because they had not been paid. They threatened to hold him hostage until they got their money. Durant wired for $300,000, which was rushed to him by train; paid off the crew, and was allowed to join the ceremony.

As a band played music, a Chinese crew brought forth the last spike, made of solid gold. Governor Leland Stanford of California started to drive the golden spike into the tie with a silver hammer, but the hammer kept sliding off the spike. Finally Jack Casement, the work boss of the Union Pacific crew, drove the spike in. (Stanford had it removed the next day. He was afraid someone would try to steal it.) The United States was now linked by rail from one end of the continent to the other. Industrialization had triumphed over the American wilderness.

Portrait of Allan Pinkerton, the private detective who chased the James Gang for almost twenty years but failed to catch them.

6
Robbing
the Railroad

"There is a hell of an excitement
in this part of the country"

The railroad boom in the American West and Midwest had one consequence that few people anticipated: It gave birth to the train robber. On October 6, 1866, the first train robbery in American history took place. Three masked men, John and Simeon Reno and Franklin Sparks, boarded an Ohio and Mississippi train outside of Seymour, Indiana. They knocked the guard out, pushed two safes containing a total of $45,000 off the train, and escaped.

After the Renos' success, others began to imitate them. Two young outlaws foolishly made the mistake of holding up a train in the Renos' territory. Infuriated, the Renos rode out after the two, caught them, robbed them of the money they had stolen, beat them, and then turned them over to a local sheriff!

Before they pulled their first train robbery, the Reno Gang, as they called themselves, had terrorized Clinton County in Indiana. There were at least eight members of the gang, and they controlled the town of Seymour. Nothing happened in their territory without their approval. Had the Renos not turned to train robbery, they might have lived to a ripe old age as bandits. But they made a final mistake when they robbed a train that was under the protection of the Pinkerton Detective Agency. The agency, run by Allan Pinkerton, its founder, along with his sons William and Robert, was famous for its tenacity in pursuing criminals. Their motto, "The Eye That Never Sleeps," led to private detectives' being called private eyes. They were notified of the train robbery and immediately set out in pursuit of the Reno Gang.

Because the gang was well protected in Seymour, Pinkerton decided to kidnap John Reno, who was the oldest brother and the gang leader. He planned to jail Reno in another town and then arrange for a speedy trial. Even though Pinkerton knew that what he was doing was illegal, he firmly believed the ends justified the means. Whenever he felt handicapped by the law, he was willing to bend it in his favor.

Pinkerton knew that the local people liked to gather at the train station to watch the express pass by. He had arranged for a bartender who worked for him to make friends with Reno and then take him to the station to watch the express. However, Pinkerton secretly arranged for another train to arrive a few minutes before the express was due. This train would be carrying him and his men. The people of Seymour would not know that this was a special train arriving early. They would think it was the express. In this way, Pinkerton would be able to surprise John Reno before he knew what was happening.

As Pinkerton's train came around a bend and stopped at the station, six men jumped off and surrounded the outlaw, who Pinkerton recognized from a picture. Before he could draw his guns, they carried him screaming and kicking to their train as an astonished crowd watched. He was quickly tried, found guilty, and sentenced to prison.

Robbing the Railroad

Shortly afterward, three other Reno brothers—William, Simeon, and Frank—and their gang robbed another train outside of Seymour. The train's engineer and the messenger guarding the safe were beaten unconscious and the conductor was shot down when he opened fire on the outlaws. The gang rode off with $96,000 and immediately split up. William Pinkerton first tracked down three gang members who had fled to Illinois and captured them without difficulty. When the Pinkerton detectives arrived at the Seymour train station with their prisoners, it was late at night. Danger seemed to be in the air. The detectives put their prisoners in a wagon and set out for a nearby town, guns drawn in case some of the outlaws' friends should try to rescue them. Suddenly they were confronted by a vigilante committee of two hundred masked riders. The leader ordered the Pinkerton guards to return to town. The vigilantes, afraid that the outlaws might gain their release, took the law into their own hands. They dragged the outlaws to the nearest tree and promptly hanged them.

Soon after the lynchings other Pinkerton agents arrested William and Simeon Reno along with several gang members and took them to the town of Lexington, Indiana, for trial. Hundreds of vigilantes gathered to lynch the prisoners, and the governor was forced to call out the militia. The Reno brothers and other gang members were transferred to another jail for safety and were kept there until Allan Pinkerton could bring back the last gang members, who had fled to Canada.

Pinkerton located Frank Reno and the rest of the outlaws outside of Windsor, Ontario, and arrested them. As Canada was considering a request for extradition, Pinkerton traveled back and forth between Detroit and Windsor on a ferry. On one such trip Pinkerton heard a click directly behind him. His instinct told him someone was cocking a revolver at his head. Whirling around, he caught the gunman's hand

and put his finger in the trigger guard so the gun could not be fired. He wrestled the gun away from his would-be killer, and after a brief, violent fight, subdued him. Two days later, in Detroit, another gunman shot at Pinkerton but missed.

Finally Canada agreed to extradite the last members of the Reno Gang on the condition that they be protected from a lynch mob. On December 7, 1868, the engineer who had been severely beaten by the Renos during the train robbery died from his wounds. An unnatural quiet settled over the town. At midnight of December 12–13, a large group of masked men moved quietly into town. The group went to the jail and warned the two deputies inside that unless they opened the door, they would be hanged with the Renos. The deputies yielded and the vigilantes entered. Holding their torches high, the mob searched the cells for the Renos and the rest of the gang, while the other prisoners crouched in fear. The outlaws were dragged to the upper tier of the jail, where ropes were thrown around the rafters and the nooses placed around the necks of the men. One by one, the men were thrown off the upper level. But their necks did not break and they slowly strangled. When one gang member, Charlie Anderson, was thrown off the tier, the noose slipped from his neck and he crashed to the floor below. Screaming for mercy, he was dragged

Jesse James.

88

upstairs and hanged again. This time, they let him down easy so the noose wouldn't slip. Simeon was also hanged in the same way, but after the vigilantes left, he regained consciousness. As the other prisoners in the jail watched in horror from their locked cells, Simeon desperately tried to free himself. But his feet just missed touching the floor by inches, and for thirty minutes, he hung in the air, struggling frantically as the life was strangled from him.

Perhaps the most famous group of train robbers were the James-Younger Gang, composed of Frank and Jesse James, Cole Younger, and Younger's three brothers. They were all pro-Southern farmers from Missouri who hated the North. During the Civil War, all of them had ridden with Quantrill's Raiders, a group of Southern guerrillas who terrorized Union sympathizers and supporters in Kansas and Missouri, massacring soldiers and civilians alike. They were a violent, vicious, bloody band who often used the war as an excuse to carry out all sorts of atrocities. When the war ended, the Youngers and the Jameses tried to return to their life as farmers but encountered much hostility from those who had supported the North. The former raiders turned to the outlaw life, which seemed to suit them well, and the James and Younger boys became legendary outlaws and killers throughout the West for almost eighteen years.

Frank James.

The Iron Horse

In 1873 the James brothers pulled their first train robbery. Learning that a train carrying $75,000 in gold was headed toward Chicago, they planned to ambush, wreck, and then rob it in Iowa. Choosing a remote spot, they loosened a rail and tied a rope around it. When the train approached, the robbers pulled the rail away from the track. The locomotive plunged off its track and rolled over on its side, crushing the engineer to death. The robbers boarded the train, shooting in the air and terrifying the passengers and crew, but injuring no one inside the train. But when the safe was opened, there was only $3,000 in it. The James Gang had robbed the wrong train.

Some time afterward, the police learned that Frank and Jesse James were hiding at their mother's house. The local sheriff and his deputies, led by two unidentified men, believed to be William Pinkerton and one of his agents, surrounded the house. Unknown to them, the James brothers had left, leaving behind Jesse's mother, Zerelda; a Dr. Samuels, who was a friend of the family; and Jesse's two small half brothers. The two detectives crept up to the house to see what was going on. When they were spotted, they tossed a flare into the house, hoping it would drive everyone out into the arms of the waiting posse. Unfortunately, the doctor pushed the flare into the fireplace, where it exploded, injuring eight-year-old Archie and shredding the arm of Jesse's mother. Archie died several days later and Jesse's mother lost her arm. Out of this incident the myth was born that the James Gang robbed trains because of what the railroad did to their family. There was no truth to it. They robbed trains for the same reason they robbed banks—because that's where the money was.

The Reno brothers and the James-Younger Gang were among the first to rob trains. But they certainly weren't the last. From 1870 on, almost every railroad in the United States was robbed at one time or another. The railroads tried to fight back. They hired detective

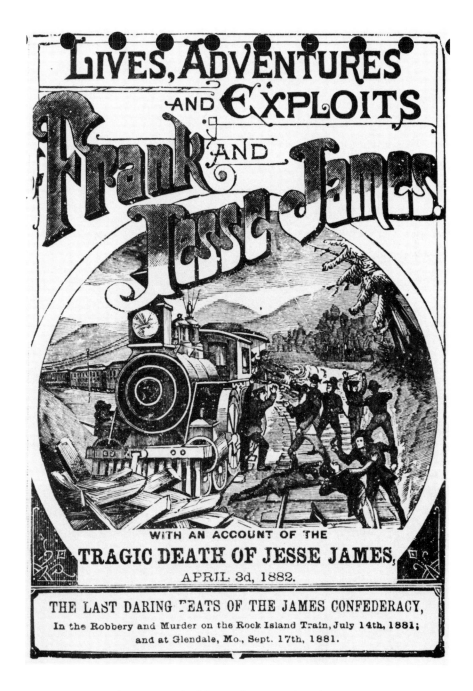

WITH AN ACCOUNT OF THE

TRAGIC DEATH OF JESSE JAMES,

APRIL 3d, 1882.

THE LAST DARING FEATS OF THE JAMES CONFEDERACY,

In the Robbery and Murder on the Rock Island Train, July 14th, 1881;
and at Glendale, Mo., Sept. 17th, 1881.

A magazine cover showing a holdup of a train by the James-Younger Gang.

agencies such as Pinkerton's to guard their lines and track down train robbers. They built reinforced express cars in which to protect the money they shipped. And they had special safes built that were supposed to be outlaw-proof. Nothing worked. Whenever train robbers were caught or killed, others took their place. When detectives sat at both ends of the train with rifles, imaginative train robbers managed to climb on the roof of the train and swing themselves down into the baggage car. When doors were made of reinforced steel, train robbers used dynamite. In one train robbery carried out by Butch Cassidy and the Sundance Kid, the leaders of the famous Hole-in-the-Wall Gang, the guard refused to open the door to the car carrying the money. The gang placed dynamite in the lock and blew the door off. And when the guard refused to open the safe, they blew the safe open with dynamite too.

Train robbers couldn't afford to sit around and count their loot. They were immediately chased down by posses, many of whose members were more interested in the reward offered for the outlaws' capture than in justice. Some gangs had hideouts so well protected that no posse would dare to follow them there. The Hole-in-the-Wall Gang got its name from one such hideout in Wyoming. It was called the Hole-in-the-Wall because the gang hid in a canyon that could only be entered through a small pass in the wall of cliffs that surrounded it. It provided a natural fort, and any sheriff's posse that tried to enter was invariably shot down.

Chasing outlaws was a pretty risky business. Most outlaws were expert shots. Some, like Rube Burrows, were marksmen. It was claimed that Burrows could hit a knot in a tree a hundred yards away. When one posse chased him after a train robbery, he killed two men and wounded two others, one seriously. When the sheriff sent dogs to track him down, he picked off the dogs one by one. He was finally killed in a gun battle with a storekeeper.

Sometimes a train robber, seeing that there was no hope of escaping from a posse, would turn and attack his pursuers, taking as many with him as he could before he himself was killed. Other times, a robber who had been wounded would shoot himself or be shot by one of the gang. One wounded robber was shot in the head by a gang leader, who said: "Dead men can't talk to detectives."

Perhaps the wildest chase in the history of train robberies was that involving Oliver Curtis Perry. Perry had managed to fix a rope ladder to the top of a railway car in which money was stored in a safe. It was February and quite cold, and as the train sped down the tracks Perry climbed the ladder and hung on. From time to time, half-frozen from cold, Perry peered into the window to see if the right moment had come for him to shoot through the glass and enter the car. Finally, he broke the window with his gun and wounded the guard, who managed to sound the alarm before he collapsed. Perry then put on a disguise and walked off the train when it stopped, but he was recognized and a chase began. Running down the tracks, Perry jumped on a freight train. Forcing the engineer to uncouple the locomotive, he began to drive it down the tracks. The engineer of the train he had tried to rob uncoupled *his* locomotive and began to chase Perry on another track with a number of passengers aboard armed with shotguns. The passenger locomotive was faster than the freight and soon overtook it. Perry then put the freight locomotive in reverse. The engineer did the same with his locomotive. For the next fifteen minutes, the two locomotives passed each other back and forth on the track, the passengers firing at Perry each time they passed and Perry firing back. Finally, as his locomotive was losing steam, Perry jumped off and tried to escape in the darkness but was caught by an unarmed deputy sheriff.

As dramatic as train robberies were, they were seldom violent. As long as the victims complied, the train robbers didn't injure them. Some holdup men were particularly respectful to women and would never rob them. Train robberies also had their moments of humor. In one holdup, the outlaws found that they had stopped a train carrying about a hundred Chinese workers who didn't understand a word of English. When told to put their hands up, the Chinese looked confused, and ignoring the outlaws, chatted away in Chinese. One of the gang finally got their attention when he fired his pistol over their heads. Two hundred hands shot up in the air, and the train robbers proceeded to take all their possessions from them. In another train robbery, Butch Cassidy held his pistol to the head of the agent guarding the safe and threatened to blow it off if he didn't open the safe. The guard stubbornly refused. Cassidy admired his courage and didn't kill him. The gang then took a vote on whether or not to rob the passengers. The vote was against it. So the robbers jumped off the train and rode off. And finally, one gang of train robbers was considerate enough of the media to leave a press release behind with the conductor after they robbed a train. It read as follows:

> The most daring robbery on record! The Southland train on the Iron Mountain Railroad was stopped here this evening and robbed of $5000. The robbers arrived at the station a few minutes before the arrival of the train and arrested the stationmaster and put him under guard. The robbers were large men, none under six feet. They were all

masked and rode fine blooded horses. There is a hell of an excitement in this part of the country.

The oldest train robber in American history was probably Bill Miner, who started his career as an outlaw in 1866, when he robbed his first stagecoach at the age of twenty-one. In the 1880s he was robbing trains as the head of a small gang. In 1901, at the age of fifty-six, he escaped from prison and continued his career as an outlaw. In 1911, when he was in his mid-sixties, Miner held up a railroad in Georgia and robbed the safe of $3,000. His hair had turned white and his hand so trembled with arthritis that the messenger was afraid the gun would go off accidentally. But the man who successfully escaped posses and lynch mobs throughout his life was trapped by the telephone. Word was quickly passed to sheriffs in the surrounding states, and Miner was eventually caught hiding in the woods of West Virginia. When he finally realized there was no escape, he reportedly told his captors, "You know, I'm getting too old for this kind of work."

American express train, late 1800s. (The New York Public Library)

7
The Romance
of the Railroad

"We talked railroads,
we dreamed railroads,
we lived railroads"

The railroad revolutionized life in America. It changed the way people traveled, the way they did business, and the way they thought about the world and organized their lives. The federal government encouraged these changes by supporting new railroads. By 1871, the government had given away over 160 million acres in land grants to railroads, an area equal in size to California and Nevada combined. Total railroad mileage increased from 35,000 after the Civil War to 93,000 by 1880. By 1900, the figure would reach 193,000. The Dakotas had six railroads, some serving towns with as few as six people. Nebraska had nine and Kansas fourteen. Every town felt that in order to survive it needed a branch line that would connect it with the main route. Railroads began to auction off feeder lines to towns, awarding a line to the highest bidder. As a result, many communities went broke, were unable to generate enough business to pay for the cost of the line.

An 1878 United States government map marking lands granted to railroad

DEPARTMENT OF THE INTERIOR
U.S GEOGRAPHICAL AND GEOLOGICAL SURVEY OF THE ROCKY MOUNTAIN REGION
J. W. POWELL, IN CHARGE

MAP OF THE UNITED STATES

EXHIBITING THE GRANTS OF LANDS MADE BY THE GENERAL GOVERNMENT
TO AID IN THE CONSTRUCTION OF RAILROADS AND WAGON ROADS
1878

See explanation see chapter on "Land Grants in aid of Internal Improvements"

The base chart was engraved for the Statistical Atlas of the United States.

companies. (The New York Public Library)

The Iron Horse

In the West, the successful completion of the transcontinental railroad led to a boom in the construction of new lines. Of the 35,000 miles of track laid down in the decade after the Civil War, almost two-thirds was west of the Mississippi River. Among the more famous lines were the Kansas Pacific and Great Northern railroads built by Henry Villard and James Hill, which opened up the Pacific Northwest. Villard was a liberal and progressive thinker from Germany who built the Kansas Pacific Railroad with the intention of making it a profitable first-rate line. When he completed it in 1883, he invited hundreds of famous people to attend the ceremony. The event was written up in all the newspapers. *The New York Times* said, "A wilderness is now open to civilization and one which is adequate to support in comfort the surplus population in Europe."

With the increase in the number of lines, railroads began to make a major effort to attract passengers. They made travel into a luxury experience rather than an ordeal. The Central Pacific Railroad took advantage of its route through the Sierra Nevada of California; from comfortable seats, passengers watched spectacular views of high-ranging mountains with snow-covered peaks, and deep canyons with winding rivers.

Another "entertainment" offered to railroad passengers in the West was the senseless slaughter of animals from moving trains. Whenever deer, buffalo, or coyotes were spotted, men would line up on the open-air platform at the rear of the train and fire at them with their rifles and pistols. In the beginning, some of the slaughtered animals were used for food, since the first trains did not provide meals or rest stops. But more often than not, the killing of animals was wanton, as was typical of the nineteenth-century West. At times, the trains would even stop to allow the passengers to get out and kill hundreds of animals for sheer amusement, leaving the bodies piled up

A buffalo slaughter from a moving train. The animals were killed for "sport."
The killings created starvation among Native Americans, who depended on
the buffalo for food and clothing.

at the side of the tracks, while Native Americans, whose battles with the railroads had ended in defeat, looked on with grief and amazement.

One major change in railroads was in food service and passenger accommodations. Before the Civil War, most trains did not serve meals and allowed only ten minutes for meals every eight or ten hours so that passengers usually had to bolt down greasy, ill-prepared food. One man who helped change this was Fred Harvey, a restaurant owner who had a simple formula for success: good food served by attractive waitresses. He convinced the Atchison, Topeka & Santa Fe Railroad to allow him to set up a chain of restaurants at various stops along the line. They were an instant success. So were the waitresses. The Harvey Girls, as they were then called, became legendary throughout the West and over half of them married railroad men.

But the man who revolutionized railroad comfort was George Pullman, whose specially built dining and sleeping cars became the standard of the day. Pullman, a hard-hearted man who had worked his way up from poverty, had good taste and a sense of comfort and luxury. Railroads leased his coaches and charged $2.00 extra to ride in them, which many passengers willingly paid. Some Pullman coaches were compared to palaces. They were built with the finest mahogany wood and had seats of plush velvet. Some cars contained comfortable, couchlike seats that converted into sleeping berths at night. There were upper and lower berths, and passengers in the upper berths climbed in and out on a ladder. All dressing and undressing took place inside the berths.

For those who could afford it, combination private bedrooms and parlor compartments were available. One passenger, the Reverend David Macrae, described riding in one of these suites:

Harried travelers in 1886 bolt their food at a depot lunchroom during a brief station stop. Sometimes lunchroom owners bribed trainmen to leave the station early so food left uneaten could be resold to the next hungry crowd. The cartoonist's unflattering portrayal of African-American workers is evidence of the racial attitudes of the day. (The New York Public Library)

A sleeping car, one of the major changes in railroad travel after the Civil War. The man who brought comfort to travel was George Pullman, who designed both sleeping and dining cars.

The discomforts of travel: weary passengers settling for the night. (The New York Public Library)

The parlor is furnished with a richly cushioned sofa and chairs, a stove, gilded racks for parcels and books and a table at which you can sit and write or have your meals. The conductor, who awakes you in the morning, brings in your breakfast and the morning papers. . . . It is a little like a traveling hotel.

The dining room served the finest food and drink. Glasses were made of crystal, and the dinnerware was solid silver. All porters and waiters were black. George Pullman made it a practice to hire only black men as porters, not for humanitarian reasons but probably because he could pay them low wages. Their income came primarily from tips. They worked long hours—porters were always on twenty-four-hour call—and they had to follow rigorous rules of how to conduct themselves and provide service. The porter was considered a servant whose only purpose on the train was to serve the passenger. He had to answer all calls courteously and promptly, and put up with abuse, which he encountered fairly often. Some passengers, especially if they had been drinking, would play practical jokes on him or curse him with racial slurs. Porters were seldom called by their real names and never addressed as Mister. Most people called porters George—probably after George Pullman.

Yet even though they were exploited, thousands of black people found employment with the railroad during a period of American history when they were constantly denied jobs throughout the United States. A steady job on the railroad, despite its long hours and low pay, enabled many porters and waiters to marry, own their own homes, and send their sons and daughters to college, providing the black community with a new generation of leaders.

Also servicing nineteenth-century railroads were news butchers—young boys who worked the trains selling everything from magazines and newspapers to candy, fruit, and soda. Many of them made extra money by selling racy material on the side to traveling salesmen or bachelors.

For most railroads, glamorous trains were not enough. They needed glamorous train stations as well. The stations seemed more like castles or Roman temples or even churches; soon the most elaborate building in most towns was the train station. The station was a testimony to the world that the town was important, worthy of having a railroad in its center.

As the number of trains increased, railroads could no longer afford to be sloppy about schedules. They had to depart and arrive on time, and as a result they changed the way America kept time. Before 1883, almost all cities and many small towns had their own notion about the correct time. Often a local jeweler would determine the right time. When it was noon in Chicago, it was 12:31 in Pittsburgh, 12:24 in Cleveland, 12:13 in Cincinnati, 12:09 in Louisville, 12:07 in Indianap-olis, and 11:50 in St. Louis. In the state of Michigan, there were twenty-seven different local times; there were thirty-eight in Wiscon-sin and twenty-three in Indiana. A traveler who journeyed from Eastport, Maine, to San Francisco, California, would have to change his watch twenty times during the trip. To show differences in local time, some railroad stations had a number of clocks. The station at Buffalo had three and the Pittsburgh station six.

Before the railroads, it really didn't matter too much what time it was, because people lived life according to the rhythms of nature. They arose with the sun and went to bed shortly after dark. Stage-coaches and boats had general schedules, but they were never very reliable. In those days, however, people were seldom in a hurry. It was an era when a letter could take weeks to travel from one part of the country to another.

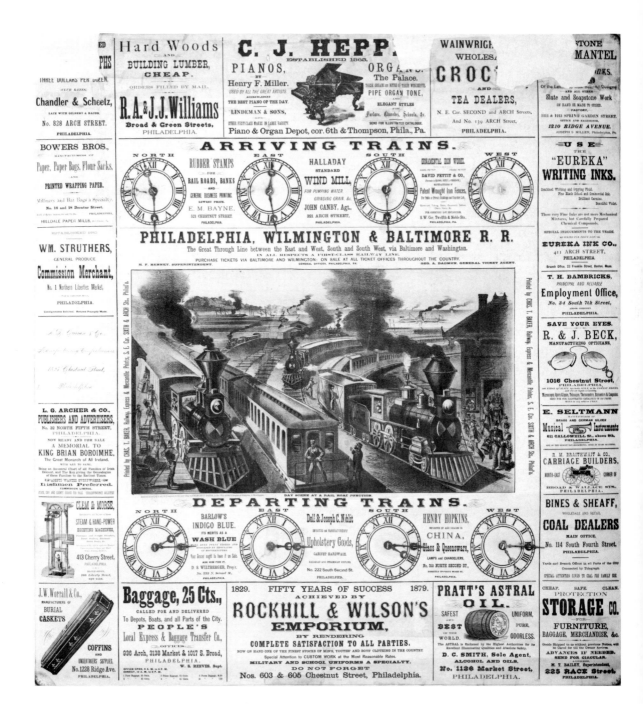

Philadelphia train schedule, 1879.

The Iron Horse

At first the railroads operated the same way. The schedules, when there were any, were very general and nobody, not even the train crew, knew exactly what time a train would arrive and when it would depart. The public expressed its irritation by renaming the railroads according to the way they behaved. The Delaware, Lackawanna and Western Railroad, or the D, L & W as it was called, was known to its riders as the Delay, Linger and Wait. As the number of lines multiplied, this disorder had to end. Railroads needed to move at exact times in order to keep the traffic flowing and avoid accidents. An organization set up by the U.S. government called the General Time Convention organized four time zones across the country: Eastern, Central, Mountain, and Pacific. Each zone was one hour different from the zone on either side of it, and every community within a zone set its clocks to the same time. One newspaper, the *Indianapolis Sentinel*, remarked: "People will have to marry by railroad time and die by railroad time. Ministers will be required to preach by railroad time and banks will open and close by railroad time."

And Henry Thoreau noted: "They come and go with such regularity and precision, and their whistle can be heard so far off, that farmers set their clocks by them, and thus one well-regulated institution regulates the whole country."

The railroads not only changed the way people traveled and regulated their schedules. They changed the economy of the country and the way people did business. They carried goods farther and faster than any other means of transportation. Trains brought wheat, corn, and hogs from the farms of the Midwest to eastern cities in such large quantities that agriculture became a major business. Texans saw that the railroad gave them the opportunity to ship their cattle to eastern markets. First they had to drive them a thousand miles north, over prairielands once grazed by buffalo, to waiting railroad cars at Abi-

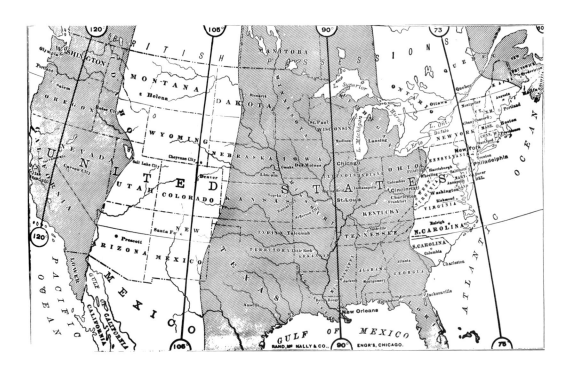

Map showing the divisions of the country into standard time zones.

An 1884 cartoon entitled "A Wild-Cat Train, No Stop Overs." (Currier & Ives lithograph, The New York Public Library)

lene, Kansas. These cattle drives became part of the western legend. The cowboys ran their herds along the Chisholm and other famous trails, fought Indians and outlaws, and weathered cattle stampedes and droughts to bring their beef to market. The cattle towns, such as Abilene and Dodge City, became famous for their marshals and outlaws. Gunfights were common, and lawmen like Wyatt Earp and Bat Masterson were hired to tame the towns. By 1880 more than four million head of cattle had been run northward over the cattle trails before farmers put up fences and sheep herders turned their flocks loose to graze the land. These forces ended the cattle drives.

Trains made it possible for industry to grow and consolidate. It was now convenient to bring raw materials into a factory and ship finished products out. Pittsburgh became one of the most powerful producers of steel in the country, as railroads transported millions of tons of coal from West Virginia and Pennsylvania mines for its furnaces and carried the finished steel products all over America. Some industrial barons controlled both an industry and the railroad that shipped its products. One of the more successful industrial leaders of this kind was Franklin Gowen, whose railroad, the Pennsylvania and Reading Coal and Iron, owned rich coal-lands in Pennsylvania and monopolized the transportation of coal out of the region.

But perhaps the deepest impact the railroads made on nineteenth-century America was in the minds of the people. Railroads captured the public's imagination. The steam engine was the symbol of the age and of the power of industrialism. "We talked railroads, we dreamed railroads, we lived railroads," one woman wrote in her diary. To a young boy growing up in the golden age of railroads, the locomotive engineer was a hero, roaring down the track behind his powerful engine, surrounded by a cloud of steam, blowing the whistle. He was such an exalted figure that no one ever dared to address him by his first name. Nor did an engineer ever use his first name. He would use the initials of his first and middle name. Thus, Charles William Smalls was called C. W. Smalls and George Benjamin Carruthers was known as G. B. Carruthers.

But the romance of the railroad was often far removed from reality. Railroads were a business and the men who built them were mainly interested in making fortunes, even if it was at the expense of their own railroads. As we have seen, Thomas Durant and Collis Huntington made huge fortunes by overcharging for building the transcontinental railroad, which they burdened with enormous debt. Others, like Jay Gould, approached a railroad like a vulture approaching a wounded animal. He would pick it clean before getting rid of its body. One of his victims was the Union Pacific. By 1880 over a hundred railroads had gone bankrupt. Most of them had overcapitalized, which meant that they sold far more stocks and bonds than the railroad was worth. When they couldn't pay their debts, they collapsed, causing thousands of people to lose their money.

The railroad barons realized that if they were to survive, they had to take drastic action. To increase their profit, they focused on two things—increasing rates when they could and paying as little as possible to their workers. Both acts were to cost the railroads millions of dollars, and hundreds of people their lives.

Collis Huntington, president of the Southern Pacific, considered to be one of the most ruthless railroad barons of his day.

8
The Railroad
Robs the People

"As much as the traffic will bear"

Collis Huntington knew that his railroad was in trouble. The novelty of transcontinental travel had soon worn off and the Central Pacific began to lose large sums of money.

Revenues dropped. At one point, Huntington and his associates tried to sell the railroad but no one wanted to buy it. The $20 million price was too high. It was then that Huntington began to carry out a plan that made him seem, according to one newspaper, "as ruthless as a crocodile." He decided to gain a monopoly of all transportation in California. He quickly took control of several smaller railroad lines and changed his company's name to the Southern Pacific. In order to end the freight competition from steamships (many merchants shipped their freight to the East Coast by boat because it was much cheaper than rail), Huntington threatened to raise their rates. He then began to squeeze his customers, charging them "as much as the traffic could bear." The railroad even determined how much profit they could make. Any money above that went to pay increased freight charges. When gold miners began to ship gold on his freight trains, he first charged them $50 a car, then $73, then $100. When they complained, they were told by railway officials: "We can't ship high-grade ore on low-grade rates." The railroad arrogantly asked to examine the miners' books in order to tell them how much money they could make. The miners angrily refused and finally settled for a rate of $73.

Part of the problem was that the railroad was in constant need of money. It was burdened by enormous debts and expenses. Huntington did everything in his power to keep the cash coming in. He bribed and lied, broke the law, and destroyed those who opposed him. This was the way business was done in the nineteenth century—like a street fight with no holds barred.

Huntington perfected the art of pressuring communities to pay him to have the railroad pass through the area. If a town wanted a railroad, it had to pay him a cash fee and give him free land. Otherwise, he would route the railroad through another town that would pay. If there was no other community, he would build one. Most towns could not resist the pressure, for to do so would be economic suicide. To prosper and attract business, a town had to have a railroad.

When people protested and sought legislative action against Huntington's ruthless practices, they found that he had bought and paid for the legislators; when they took him to court, they found that he had bought and paid for the judges. Anyone he couldn't buy he characterized as a "wild hog" and did his best to destroy.

The Southern Pacific's policies were so harsh that they caused a war to break out in the San Joaquin Valley between the railroad and the farmers. The railroad, in need of money and wanting to develop land it owned, tried to attract farmers to settle in the valley. The railroad promised to sell them the land at a future date at a price of

$2.50 to $5.00 an acre. The railroad also promised it would not consider any improvements made on the land as part of its value. However, the railroad did not guarantee that it would do what it promised.

The valley was a parched land without trees, water, or materials to build homes. It was burning hot and plagued with dust storms in the summer; it was freezing cold in the winter. But the settlers were determined people and the soil was potentially rich. They ate jackrabbits, brought water from a nearby lake to irrigate the land, and turned it into a rich and fertile valley filled with shade trees, fruit orchards, vegetables, and wheat.

In 1877, the Southern Pacific decided to sell the land. But instead of selling it to the farmers who worked it, the railroad offered the valley to the highest bidder at $40 and $50 an acre. In addition, all the improvements the farmers had made with their own hard labor—including their orchards, fields, and irrigation systems—would be sold by the railroad at the railroad's price. The farmers considered this a violation of their understanding with the railroad and revolted. They formed an organization called the Settlers' League. Its members wore masks, carried out military drills, and had secret meetings. The League took its case to the California courts, where they lost, as the courts were controlled by Huntington. They appealed the case to the Supreme Court. In the meantime, anyone who moved in was threatened by the Settlers' League and forced to leave.

The railroad then hired two gunmen named Hart and Crowe, promising them free farms as long as they could hold the property against the Settlers' League. The sheriff accompanied them to evict the owners at a place called Mussel Slough. The Settlers' League quickly arrived on the scene, told the sheriff that the case was before the Supreme Court, and asked him to leave peacefully and not take any action until the court made its ruling. The sheriff agreed. But Hart and Crowe suddenly reached for their guns and began to fire at the farmers. Six settlers were killed and one was wounded. Both Hart and Crowe were killed. The railroad immediately characterized the incident as an insurrection, but the truth quickly came out. It did not help the families of the dead men or the farmers of the region. They were forced out of their homes and left the valley. Some years later, in another valley, another organization faced with the same problems took its case to the Supreme Court and won. The Southern Pacific had to sell them the land at the agreed-upon price of $2.50 to $5.00 an acre.

Several years after the Mussel Slough tragedy, two masked train robbers, one tall, the other short, climbed into the cab of a Southern Pacific train and ordered the engineer at gunpoint to stop. They then ordered the guard in the express car to open the door or throw out the safe. He refused to do either. The robbers then placed dynamite under the express car and lit it, blowing the car off the tracks and onto its side. Again they ordered the expressman to open the door. Again he refused. Finally, they told him that if he continued to refuse they would shoot the engineer and fireman. The door opened and out came the safe. The robbers blew it open and rode off with $5,000.

From that time on, Southern Pacific trains were periodically held up by a short and tall masked duo. As hard as they tried, railroad detectives and police were unable to find the slightest clue as to the identity of the two men. The people so hated the railroad that no one would cooperate with the police. The detectives became so frustrated that they arrested a number of men, including two of the infamous Dalton brothers, the leaders of a band of bank and train robbers who had moved to California. There was absolutely no evidence to connect

Southern Pacific trains passing through the San Joaquin Valley. The farmers in this valley revolted against the railroad when it tried to cheat them out of their land.

the Daltons to the train robbery, but the Southern Pacific cared little for evidence. Its only concern was to make an arrest, whether or not those arrested were guilty or innocent.

One day one of the detective agencies assigned to the case heard that a man by the name of George Sontag had been talking freely about the robberies and about his brother John and a friend of his brother's by the name of Chris Evans. Both men had grievances against the Southern Pacific. Sontag had been a brakeman but was crippled in an accident while working for the railroad. And the family of Evans's wife had been evicted from Southern Pacific land.

George Sontag was an unreliable witness and there was no evidence linking his brother and Evans to the holdups. But two detectives were sent to Evans's house to question him. As they approached the house, it happened that they saw John Sontag enter through the back way. The detectives burst in through the front door, and finding Chris Evans's sixteen-year-old daughter, Eve, alone, they began to question her about Sontag. Without identifying themselves, they rudely asked Eve where Sontag was now. Unaware that he had entered the house, she replied that she didn't know. When one of the detectives called her a "damned liar" she ran and told her father what was happening. He grabbed a gun and returned to the house. There was a blast of gunfire and the two detectives fled, one seriously wounded. Evans and Sontag immediately took for the woods.

For eighteen months, the railroad and the local sheriffs searched the woods for the two men. Even though they occasionally found them, Evans and Sontag always managed to shoot their way out, wounding and, at times, killing members of the posse. Most of the time, they hid with loggers and miners, men who had no love for the railroad and who never asked the fugitives any questions about who they were and why they were there. At one time there were so many deputies in the woods searching for Evans and Sontag that the posses began to accidentally shoot each other. Eleven men were wounded.

As the chase dragged on, most people rooted for the two outlaws. But eventually the law caught up with them. As they were making their way to a cabin in the woods, a sheriff's posse ambushed them. Both men were wounded. Sontag was so filled with bullets he could not move. He was captured, and died shortly afterward. Evans was shot in the left arm and left eye. He managed to escape for a short time, but, because his wounds were so serious, he gave himself up. He was taken to a hospital, where his left arm was removed, and then he was taken to jail.

As Evans was awaiting trial, someone smuggled a gun to him and he escaped. This time, the sheriff decided to trap Evans through deceit rather than send another posse after him. He managed to get a counterfeit note to Evans from his daughter that said that one of his children was seriously ill and that he should come at once. Evans fell for the trick and was captured as he returned home. He was sent to prison for twenty years, but fifteen years later the governor of California, Hiram Johnson, who hated the Southern Pacific, pardoned him. Evans never admitted or even hinted that he and Sontag had held up the railroad. Nor was there any evidence to show that they ever did. It may have all been a tragic mistake.

Huntington's ruthless methods cost the railroad nothing but ill will. The severest criticism of the railroad came from the novelist Frank Norris, who wrote a fictionalized version of the Mussel Slough tragedy in his novel *The Octopus*. In the novel, there is a scene in which one of the characters, Presley, sees a train run over a flock of sheep at night without bothering to stop. This event makes him aware of the brutal nature of the railroad. Norris describes Presley's realization of this as follows:

The Iron Horse

Presley saw again in his imagination the galloping monster, the terror of steam and steel with its single eye, red, Cyclopean . . . but he saw it now as a symbol of vast power, huge, terrible, flinging the echoes of its thunder over the reaches of the valley and leaving blood and destruction in its path; the leviathan with tentacles of steel clutching into the soil, the sullen Force, the iron-hearted Power, the monster, the Colossus, the Octopus.

Occasionally, one determined man could take on the powerful railroad and defeat it. In Oakland, California, John Davie wanted to build a warehouse to store his goods for trading. The local politicians, who were controlled by the railroad, gave him permission to build as long as he constructed his warehouse on railroad property. In this way the railroad could control the freight in and out of the warehouse and set the rate for transportation. Davie was a stubborn man. He turned down the offer and built a warehouse on state land instead. Then he went to buy coal in San Francisco to put in his warehouse and was told that the coal could not be shipped to Oakland because the railroad controlled the traffic to the city and would not ship it to him. When Davie returned to Oakland, he found a railroad wrecking crew tearing down his warehouse. When he went to stop them, the crew knocked him out with a two-by-four wooden plank. Regaining consciousness, he went to a nearby saloon for a drink, got his rifle and two pistols, and returned to the site. As soon as the wrecking crew saw him coming, they backed off and were forced to leave. Davie then recruited a group of fishermen who harvested oysters illegally (the writer Jack London was one), and who hated the railroad, to protect his property. When the police came to arrest Davie, the oystermen beat the policeman up. When the railroad sent a bargeload of thugs to attack Davie, his crew intercepted the barge and threw the thugs in the water.

Davie then became involved in a ferry company that owned the *Rosalie,* a ferry that competed against another company owned by the Southern Pacific. When the railroad ferry refused to let the *Rosalie* use the docking facility, the *Rosalie* rammed the railroad ferry onto a sandbar. Shortly afterward, a new dock was built and both ferries had to pass under a drawbridge owned by the railroad. The bridge tender refused to open the bridge to let the *Rosalie* go through. Davie had one of his men tie a rope to the bridge while he tied the other end to his ferry. The *Rosalie* then backed down the river, dragging the bridge with it. Eventually, the Southern Pacific, afraid that Davie's victories might encourage others, decided to call a truce in its war against him.

The arrogance of the Southern Pacific proves its undoing. Eventually anti-railroad politicans came to power and began to pass laws regulating it. But thousands of people suffered at its hands before the struggle ended. Farmers lost their lands, merchants their businesses, workers their jobs. The problem was not just in California. It was all over America. The late nineteenth century was an era in which industrialists ruled the country, free to do almost anything they wanted. It was the era of the robber barons, the most powerful of whom were the railroad owners, and their arrogance led to revolts by farmers and workers throughout America.

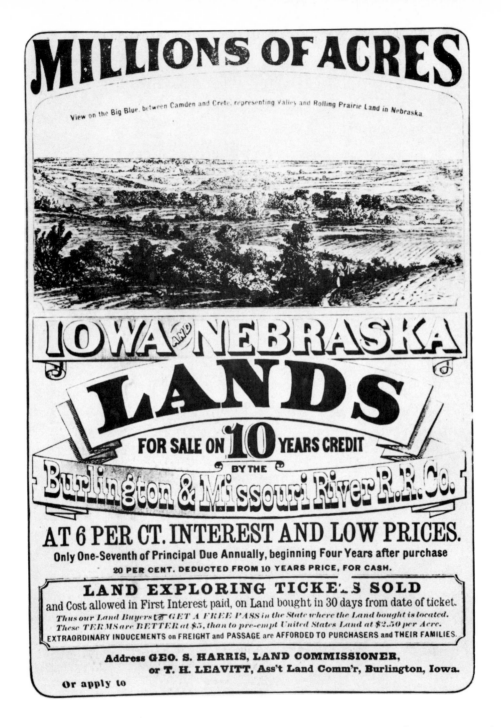

A typical advertisement for land by a railroad trying to attract farmers to settle in America. This ad was published in England.

9
The Farmers' Revolt

*"What you farmers ought to do is raise
less corn and more hell!"*

The problems that plagued the Southern Pacific Railroad in California plagued railroads throughout the Midwest, too. Despite the boom in railroad construction, there were not enough people inhabiting the land. In order for railroads to transport crops, there had to be farmers to produce them. The railroads had lots of land to sell, almost 100 million acres. Most of that was empty and a good deal of it was fertile. The problem was to convince farmers to pack up and move to the Midwest.

The railroads began to take out advertisements in newspapers throughout the United States and Europe. One railroad alone, the Union Pacific, advertised in over 2,000 newspapers. It published drawings showing pretty farmhouses with gingerbread decorations, surrounded by shade trees (the prairies didn't have trees) with horses and chickens in the yards, crops in the field, and a large barn. In the far distance was a railroad train with smoke coming from its smoke-stack. One ad read: "Millions and millions of acres of Northern Pacific

LANDS FOR SALE at the lowest prices ever offered by any railroad company ranging chiefly from $2.60 to $4.00 an acre. Best Wheat Lands Best Farming Lands Best Grazing Lands in the World."

Railroad agents also visited villages and towns in almost every country in Europe, trying to convince people to emigrate. They gave lectures, published articles in local newspapers, hung posters, and spoke with community leaders. They also lied, telling the would-be emigrants that the railroad offered free housing, fertile land, and comfortable journeys, almost none of which was ever true.

Immigrants who came over to buy land from the railroad often found themselves cheated and robbed by road agents who sold them phony train tickets to their destinations or robbed them of their possessions and money. Robert Louis Stevenson, the future author of *Treasure Island,* was one of the immigrants from England. He described Castle Garden, a place where many immigrants arrived expecting to be treated courteously and shipped to their new destination. It was a nightmare. Even cattle were treated better:

> I say that we stood like sheep, that the porters charged among us like so many sheep dogs. . . . There was no waiting room, no refreshment room, the cars were locked. . . . I sat on my valise, too crushed to observe my neighbors—but they were all cold, wet and weary and driven stupidly crazy by the mismanagement to which we had been subjected.

Once they arrived on their land, the settlers usually found life unbelievably hard. They had to contend with droughts and storms, bandits and Native Americans, sickness and wild animals. The hardest difficulties were manmade ones. The immigrants were at the mercy

A trainload of Finnish immigrants arrive in Nevada, 1880s.

of the market prices for their goods. Then they had to transport their crops at the railroad's set rates. Sometimes the railroads would wait until they saw what the market prices for the farmers' crops would be and then raise their rates at the last minute.

Another grievance farmers and merchants had against the railroad was the difference between short-haul and long-haul rates. It was often more expensive to ship something a shorter distance. That was because the railroad had competition over the long distances to major cities and had to keep rates down. But most small towns had only one line and that line could charge what it wanted. So items shipped from Chicago to a small town in California might first be shipped to San Francisco, over a thousand miles away, for $500, and then be shipped to a small town a hundred miles away for $300. Often, the train carrying the goods to a major city might pass, without stopping, through the town to which they were ultimately being delivered. The train would deliver the goods to the major city many miles away, and then the railroad would ship the goods back to the town it had just passed through, charging the person who ordered the item for the extra mileage.

Another practice that angered many people was that of rebates. If a large shipper used the line, it would often insist that the railroad return some of the money it paid if a smaller competitor also used the line. Thus, if a large steel company used the railroad and several smaller steel companies also used the same railroad, the railroad would charge the smaller companies a much higher rate than the large one and give some of the money it collected to the larger company in the form of a rebate.

Many legislators who were not on the railroad's payroll wanted to be. To pressure the railroad to bribe them, lawmakers would often introduce legislation that they knew would be burdensome to the railroad. The legislator would then announce to the world that he was protecting the people from the evils of the railroad. He would do this until someone from the railroad quietly visited him and offered him a "little gift" to forget about his bill—which the legislator would obligingly do.

This corruption angered many people, especially the farmers who suffered from the arrogance of the railroad and its attempt to squeeze every penny it could from them. The time was right for farmers to organize, and the man who would bring this about was Oliver Hudson Kelley. He was once described as "an engine with too much steam on all the time." Working as a midwestern newspaperman, Kelley traveled throughout the farmlands of the Midwest and South and became keenly aware of the farmers' sufferings at the hands of the railroads. He decided to form an organization of farmers throughout the South and Midwest for their "social and intellectual advancement." He called his organization the National Grange of the Patrons of Husbandry. At first the National Grange—or Grange, as it came to be known—was a secret society with quaint names to indicate rank. Men were called Laborers and Cultivators, Harvesters and Husbandmen; women were Maids and Shepherdesses, Gleaners and Matrons. The preamble of the Grange's constitution stated, "The soil is the source from which we derive all that constitutes wealth." Working day and night, spending his own money, writing hundreds of letters, Kelley began to contact farmers all over the country. His timing was right. Farmers eagerly responded and within a relatively short time, 20,000 lodges were formed.

But if Kelley was interested in the social and intellectual advancement of farmers, farmers were more interested in their own economic advancement. Year after year they were paid low prices for their crops and charged high shipping rates by the railroads. The Grange became

A Grange poster showing how all the professions were dependent on the

farmer for food.

the means by which the farmers organized and revolted against the railroad.

The Grange produced a number of outstanding leaders dedicated to improving the farmers' condition and forcing the railroads to establish fair rates. One of the most popular agitators was Mary Lease, a Kansas lawyer, who achieved instant fame when she yelled out during a speech, "What you farmers need to do is raise less corn and more *hell!*"

The farmers began to press state legislatures to set up railroad commissions to establish fair rates. They also pressed to end free passes and rebates, stop land grants to railroads, and in some cases, have the railroads return lands to the state. When corrupt officials refused to do so or tried to undermine their efforts, the farmers voted them out and voted in officials who would carry out their wishes. Many organized into a political party known as the Populists and elected a number of local legislators, governors, judges, and congressmen. Most midwestern states established railroad commissions that had the power to fix rates for freight and passengers. One state, Illinois, amended its constitution to read that the state "should pass laws to correct abuses . . . and extortion in the rates of freights and passenger tariffs."

The railroads fought back on a number of levels. First, they ignored the regulations—and found themselves in court. They then tried another tactic: They began to be polite to farmers, discussing farmers' grievances with them and making some adjustment in the rates. At the same time, they fought the regulations in the federal courts. In 1886, a conservative Supreme Court overturned an earlier decision in favor of the farmers and ruled that the states could not regulate a railroad that crossed state lines. Since most railroads crossed state lines, the effect was to make it almost impossible for the states to control the railroads.

However, the decision did not say that the *federal* government couldn't regulate railroads. Pressure was then put on Congress and the president, and in 1887, the first Interstate Commerce Commission (ICC) was established to regulate railroad rates throughout the country. The railroads immediately challenged it, and a highly conservative Supreme Court again decided in their favor. It was not until the twentieth century that the ICC was eventually able to set fair rates and control all railroad traffic.

But while the railroads' struggles with the farmers were slowly being resolved in state and federal regulation, its struggles with its own workers exploded into war. No industrial conflict in nineteenth-century America was more bitter or intense than the struggles that erupted between the railroads and their workers.

Scene from the Pullman strike of 1894.

10
The Railroad
Workers' Revolt

*"When we die . . . we will be buried in the Pullman
cemetery and go to the Pullman hell"*

After the end of the Civil War in 1865, a second civil war broke out
in America between the industrial barons and their workers. It was an
era when most of the owners of major industries mercilessly exploited
their workers, paying them the lowest possible wages, working them
as many hours as they could, and firing anyone who dared to organize
a union. The war between employers and workers would last for
almost eighty years, with battles fought in almost every major industry. But no battles were more bitter or deadly than those between the
railroad and its employees.

One of the first took place in the anthracite region of Pennsylvania
where coal was mined. The Pennsylvania and Reading Coal and
Iron Company owned the coal lands and the railroad by which coal
was shipped. The working conditions were brutal. Men worked
twelve hours a day, six days a week, for $10 to $35, depending upon
the job. Miners were paid by the amount of coal they dug, but the
coal was weighed on company scales rigged in favor of the railroad.

Workers were paid in scrip—"money" printed by the company—rather than in U.S. currency. The scrip could be used only in company-owned stores, which charged higher prices than regular stores and which the miners contemptuously called "gyp-me" or "pluck-me" stores.

The worst part of the job was the dangerous conditions in the mines. Men were frequently killed or maimed by falling rock, dynamite, gas explosions, and poison gases that lay hidden in the mines. During the 1870s, an average of one hundred men were killed each year in the anthracite mines, and three times as many were maimed. In one mine disaster in 1871, 111 miners died; seventeen of them were under the age of fourteen. Those who escaped violent death inside the mines usually died in agony from the dreaded black lung disease, which most miners developed because they inhaled fine particles of coal dust. This disease was a result of poor ventilation inside the mine. Once it attacked the lungs, there was no cure.

Many of the men who worked in the mines after the Civil War were Irish immigrants who had come to America to escape the harsh oppression of English rule and extreme poverty in Ireland. Because most were Catholic, poor, and uneducated, and because they had a reputation for heavy drinking and crime, they suffered from severe discrimination. People expressed their hostility openly. "No Irish need apply" was a postscript commonly added to advertisements for jobs or rooms. The Irish in the mines were often the last to be hired and the first to be fired.

To protect themselves and gain political power, in the 1860s a small group of Irish workers formed an American chapter of a secret society known as the Molly Maguires. The Mollies had originally organized in Ireland during the 1840s to battle the English landlords who oppressed Irish farmers. In America, they attacked not only those who oppressed them, but anyone with whom they had a quarrel. If a Molly was dismissed from a job, beaten in a fight, insulted, or injured, the organization sought revenge. Superintendents and foremen were killed, men brutally beaten, buildings dynamited or burned, and railroad cars overturned because some member of the Mollies had a grievance. To instill terror in their victims, the Mollies would send them "coffin notices," a sketch of a coffin indicating that the receiver could either leave town or be buried in it.

The president of the Pennsylvania and Reading, Franklin B. Gowen, was determined to crush not only the Mollies but any organization of workingmen that he felt stood in his way. Gowen turned to Allan Pinkerton to do the job.

Pinkerton quickly decided that the only way to put an end to the Mollies was to have an agent infiltrate their organization and gather evidence to convict its members. Pinkerton was too well known to do the job himself. He selected one of his detectives for the job—James McParland. McParland managed to infiltrate the Mollies and be taken in as a member of their organization. He pretended to go along with their plans to assassinate mine bosses and workers. For two years McParland gathered evidence against the group. Finally, when Jack Kehoe, the leader of the Mollies, became suspicious that he was an informer, the Pinkertons conducted a series of lightning raids in the coalfields and arrested the leaders and gang members.

On May 6, 1877, James McParland, fashionably dressed and in high spirits, entered the packed courtroom and began his testimony. Day after day, as the defendants sat shaken and stunned, McParland detailed their violent activities. He named specific killers, the times and dates of their crimes, how the plans were made, and who made them. He was a superb prosecution witness, clear and unwavering in his testimony, supplying details that only an insider could have

Scenes from the Pullman strike of 1894.

known. After McParland testified, other Mollies came out of hiding and offered to exchange information in return for their lives. At a series of subsequent trials, their testimony alone helped convict and condemn other Mollies.

On a beautiful spring day in June of 1877, nineteen young men wearing red roses and carrying crucifixes mounted the gallows. At least one was innocent; but the jury had not been careful in distinguishing the innocent from the guilty. Ten of the nineteen were hanged together in a group, including Jack Kehoe, who died a slow, horrible death when the rope around his neck slipped, slowly choking him.

As the trials of the Molly Maguires were winding down, the railroads began to have other labor troubles. In 1873, an economic depression had struck the land. Thousands of businesses had failed and millions of workers lost their jobs. Many railroads, although affected, did not suffer too greatly and even continued to pay dividends to their stockholders. A number of the lines decided to take advantage of the depression and increase their profit by cutting wages. They felt that with so many unemployed men about, they could fire any protesters and hire new men.

The workers themselves were basically unorganized. There were several unions—then called brotherhoods—of locomotive engineers, firemen, and conductors, but they were weak and ineffective. Railroads cut wages 10 percent and then an additional 10 percent. The workers accepted the cuts, feeling there was little they could do. But in 1877 when the Baltimore and Ohio Railroad announced a 10 percent cut on all wages of more than $1 a day, the firemen and brakemen immediately protested. They were unable to support their families as it was. They sent a three-man delegation to negotiate with the owners. The company took a hard line and refused to deal with them. The next day, the three were fired. Some forty firemen and brakemen refused to work and were immediately fired. New men were hired to replace them.

Word traveled up the line about what had happened, and at Martinsburg, West Virginia, the Baltimore and Ohio firemen climbed down from their engines and refused to work. They were arrested by the local police for protesting, but a sympathetic crowd surrounded the jail and they were freed. The strikers allowed passenger trains to pass, but stopped all freights. Some seventy trains carrying 1,200 freight cars were halted and turned back.

The governor of the state, John Matthews, was hot-headed and impetuous. He called out the militia, put on his uniform, and marched at the troops' head. He was determined to teach the strikers a lesson they would never forget. When he heard that the townspeople were on the side of the workers and ready for a fight, the governor quietly took off his uniform and returned home, giving up his command. Federal troops were then called in to open up the railroads and protect scabs, workers who were called in to replace the strikers. With their bayonets at the ready the troops cleared the tracks enabling two freight trains to pass safely through.

The strikers, however, were resolved to keep the strike going throughout the line. In Maryland, Governor John Carroll sent troops to the town of Camden. They ran into a mob of 2,000 angry people who began to club them and throw rocks. The troops opened fire, killing ten protesters.

The strikers tried to negotiate with the Baltimore and Ohio before the strike got worse. The railroad refused. In Pittsburgh, Pennsylvania, the workers went out on strike and the local militia did not interfere. More than 10,000 people gathered on the streets to ensure that the trains did not move. Militia units composed of a number of

Strike scenes showing the burning of the railroad yards in Pittsburgh during the railroad strike of 1877.

socially prominent young men who viewed the workers as Communists were sent in from Philadelphia. Although they were not attacked or threatened, the troops fired into the crowd, killing sixteen and wounding many women and children. A newspaper reporter described the scene:

> The sight presented after the soldiers had ceased firing was sickening. Old men and boys lay writhing in the agonies of death, while numbers of children were killed outright. The neighborhood . . . was dotted with the dead and dying while weeping women cursed loudly and deeply the instrument that made them widows, were clinging to the bleeding corpses.

The city exploded. Thousands of armed men gathered to avenge those who were killed. The troops took cover in a roundhouse, and the crowd surrounded them. Soldiers who tried to flee were immediately shot down. Mobs began to loot gun shops and set the railroads on fire. They tried to burn out the eight hundred soldiers trapped inside the roundhouse. The troops decided to make a run for it. They broke out of the roundhouse, firing as they ran, killing approximately twenty more demonstrators before reaching safety. Eight soldiers were killed.

Meanwhile the mob began to set trains and locomotives on fire. They burned more than a hundred locomotives and destroyed and looted over 3,000 freight cars. Hundreds of buildings caught or were set on fire. Ten thousand troops were called in to quiet the city. Yet even as Pittsburgh calmed down, other cities flared up. Strikes were called throughout Pennsylvania. In the city of Reading, two militia units were rushed to the city even though there was no violence. One, a militia unit composed of wealthy young men called the Easton Grays, opened fire on a peaceful gathering; they killed thirteen people and wounded thirty-two others, including five policemen. The other regiment was so infuriated that their leader angrily declared, "We will not shoot workingmen whatever the Easton Grays may do. They are our brothers and the only one we'd like to pour our bullets into is Frank Gowen, the superintendent of the Philadelphia and Reading railroad [Gowen was responsible for the prosecution of the Molly Maguires]."

The strike spread to every major city in the United States. Railroad workers blocked trains in Trenton, New Jersey; Albany and Buffalo, New York; Cincinnati, Ohio; Chicago, Illinois; Fort Wayne, Indiana; St. Louis, Missouri; and San Francisco, California. When the strike was over an estimated one hundred to two hundred people were dead and thousands were wounded. The conflict destroyed tens of millions of dollars' worth of property. While some newspapers, such as the *New York Herald*, proclaimed that "the mob is a wild beast and needs to be shot down," others, like the Chicago *Tribune*, blamed the strike on railroads:

> For years, the railroads of this country have been run outside of the United States Constitution. . . . They have charged what they pleased for fares and rates. They have corrupted the State and city legislators. They have corrupted Congress, employing for that purpose a lobby that dispensed bribes to the amount of millions. . . . Their managers have been plundering the roads . . . to their own enrichment. Finally, having nothing more to get out of the stockholders . . . they have commenced raiding . . . their own employees.

Eugene V. Debs, the great leader of the railroad union, at his desk.

Ultimately, the strikers could not withstand the power of the federal government. Those who still had their jobs drifted back to work, but thousands of men were fired and blacklisted so that they could never work for a railroad again.

Part of the reason the workers were defeated was that they were unorganized. At that time there were no strong unions to challenge the owners. After the strike, the workers began to organize along craft lines. The locomotive engineers had their own union, the foremen, brakemen, and conductors theirs. But it was hard to get the unions to work together.

It was at this point that one of the most remarkable men in American history appeared on the labor scene: Eugene V. Debs. Debs began his working career with the railroads at the age of seventeen in the city of Terre Haute, Indiana. For six years, he worked long and hard hours at a dangerous job. His mother continually begged him to quit. After a close friend of his was crushed to death by a train on which he was working, Debs left the railroad. But it would not be for long.

Shortly after he quit, Debs attended an organizational meeting of the Brotherhood of Locomotive Firemen. Debs liked what he heard and introduced himself to the speaker, who, after talking with him for several minutes, offered him the job of organizing a local chapter of the Brotherhood. He knew that no one else in the community wanted it. Debs took the job. Over the next ten years, he became a driving force in the union, recruiting thousands of men. He was so committed to his work, so honest in his way of doing things, and so straightforward in his dealings with people, that he was revered and honored by all railroad men.

Debs saw that the problem with the brotherhoods was that they were organized along craft lines. Hard as he tried, Debs could not convince the different railroad unions to unite. Finally, out of frustration, he formed the American Railway Union (ARU) in 1892 and invited all railroad workers to join together. In fact, anyone could become a member of the union if the company he worked for was owned by a railroad. Because of Debs's almost saintly personality and the fact that it was far cheaper to join his union than the brotherhoods, hundreds of thousands of workers, skilled and unskilled, joined up. Debs was so flooded with requests that he did not have enough organizers to sign workers up fast enough.

The one fault of the union was that it was racist: No blacks were allowed to join. This was a common policy of almost every union in the country. Ever since the end of the Civil War, many white workers had not only expressed a racial hatred of blacks but also feared that black workers would take whites' jobs away. Despite the fact that many blacks worked in all railroad jobs from 1830 on, by the 1890s most white railroad workers actively tried to keep blacks from working on the railroads. In many communities, but especially in the South, white workers would murder, threaten, or beat up black workers who held jobs whites wanted. Debs knew that if he tried to integrate his union at this time, it would fail. He decided not to make an issue of the matter even though he knew that racism was wrong. As a result, his union was a success. It wasn't until the mid-1920s that J. Phillip Randolph picked up where Debs left off and formed the Brotherhood of Pullman Porters to improve the working conditions for black railroad workers.

Debs also knew that it would take years before the ARU could be built up into a strong force. Unfortunately, time was not on his side. In 1893 the country was once again hit by a severe economic depression and millions of workers—perhaps as many as one out of four—

were unemployed. Again wages were cut and again railroad workers went on strike. A total of 750,000 men walked out, but only one strike was successful: the one led by Eugene Debs. The strike was against the Great Northern Railroad, owned by Jim Hill, who was a railroad baron in the mold of Collis Huntington. After Hill cut wages three times in a row, the workers revolted. Debs called a strike and all 10,000 workers went out. Not one train moved on Hill's line. Hill called the governor of the state and tried to rally the business community against Debs. But Debs was not intimidated and in fact won many of Hill's allies to his own side. Finally, Hill gave in and signed an agreement not to cut wages. The ARU was off to a great start.

Debs knew that despite the union's victory, it was still too weak for a major showdown. However, many of the members felt that they were a major force to be reckoned with. And when the employees of the Pullman Palace Car Company went out on strike in 1894, the members voted to support them, even though Debs was reluctant to do so.

The Pullman Palace

J. Phillip Randolph, the president of the Brotherhood of Pullman Porters and a civil rights leader.

Car Company, located in Chicago, Illinois, manufactured the Pullman sleeping and dining cars that were used on most passenger trains in America. Pullman himself was a typical product of nineteenth-century America. Starting with nothing but his own wits, he had an idea that he turned into a fortune: to provide luxurious and semiluxurious sleeping and eating accommodations on trains. The Pullman car became the national standard, and George Pullman made a fortune.

Pullman liked to portray himself as a friend of the workingman. In reality, when you worked in his factory, you were required to live in one of his houses, buy your groceries from his stores, send your children to his schools, and worship in his churches. If you wanted to read a book, you went to the company library, for the use of which you paid an annual fee. Pullman not only owned the factory in which "his" men and women worked, he owned the town in which they lived. As one worker described it: "We were born in Pullman's house, fed from a Pullman shop, taught in the Pullman schools and when we die . . . buried in the Pullman cemetery and go to the Pullman hell."

On the surface, the town seemed very pleasant. With its attractive and well-built homes, it seemed like a model community. But the workers had to pay rent that was at least 25 percent higher than in other places, and buy food at a higher price. Gas and water bills were 10 percent higher in Pullman's town than elsewhere. There were no saloons in the town and no trade unions were allowed. Informers were everywhere, reporting on the social and moral behavior of the inhabitants. At election time, the workers were instructed who they were expected to vote for.

As the depression of 1893 deepened, Pullman began laying off thousands of workers and cutting wages by one-third to one-half. A mechanic who worked ten hours a day for twelve days took home seven cents in his paycheck. He had earned $9.07, but the $9 was taken out for rent in advance. The only way he could eat was to draw upon credit at the company store, which meant more deductions from his paycheck. One foreman who worked 428 hours a month, averaging almost fourteen hours a day, took home $40—less than ten cents an hour. Nor did Pullman provide any pensions or disability for injured workers. A man might work thirty years in his factory and still not have job security. But to make matters worse, even as Pullman lowered wages, he raised the rents, claiming that the two businesses were separate. In desperation, the workers walked out and appealed to Debs for help. They issued a statement that read:

> We do not expect the company to concede to our demands. We do not know what the outcome will be and in fact we do not care much. We do know we are working for less wages than will maintain ourselves and our families in the necessities of life and we absolutely refuse to work any longer.

The railroad workers were eager to support the striking factory workers. Debs was not confident that his union could win this battle in such hard times. But his men were willing to fight and they vowed that they would not move any train that carried a Pullman car. A hundred thousand railroad men walked off their jobs, and trains stopped moving all over the country.

Debs had expected that the other railroad owners would support Pullman, but he felt that he could still win the strike if he received support from the brotherhoods and other unions. But many of the brotherhoods hesitated to support Debs. Their leaders resented Debs's organizing one big union that challenged their authority. Some of the leaders were also bought and paid for by the railroads. But despite the leadership's opposition, many of their rank and file walked out.

What Debs didn't anticipate was that the federal government would step in. The U.S. attorney general, Richard Olney, hated unions and sought to destroy their powers. He wanted to send federal troops to break the strike, using the excuse that the strike was preventing the mail from being delivered since the mail was carried on trains. Olney vowed to use the entire army and navy of the United States to deliver a postcard to Chicago if he had to. But the strikers were careful not to interfere with the mail.

Olney managed to get the Supreme Court to issue an injunction against the union and sent federal troops to Chicago to break the strike and move the trains. The governor of Illinois, John Altgeld, protested against using federal troops. He pointed out that there was no violence and that the situation was under the control of local authorities. But the press and business community supported the move and called Debs an anarchist and accused him of being a drunkard. Ministers preached vicious sermons against him. The Reverend Herrick Johnson encouraged violence by encouraging soldiers to "use their guns . . . and shoot to kill."

The predictable happened. In Chicago, the troops clashed with mobs—although not with the strikers themselves—killing seven people. The press attacked Debs and distorted the strike, inflaming people's feelings. Headlines ran: MOBS BENT ON RUIN; MOBS IN CONTROL; RIOT TERROR AND PILLAGE; ANARCHY IS RAMPANT. One story read:

> War of the bloodiest kind in Chicago is imminent and before tomorrow goes by the railroad lines and yards must be turned into battles strewn with hundreds of dead and wounded. . . . The anarchistic and socialist element . . .

were preparing to blow up the south end of the Federal building and take possession of millions of dollars now stored in federal vaults.

A few papers supported the strike. The *Chicago Times* characterized Pullman as "cold-hearted, cold-blooded, anti-social. He wears no mask. He has a fat face, a small pair of pudgy eyes gleam out from above puffed cheeks and the glitter of avarice is plainly apparent in their depths." The *Times* also noted that "the strike and the boycott are the only weapons left to those who had neither land nor capital but only strong hands and a willingness to work."

Soldiers threatened strikers when they refused to return to work, and even made some of them do so at the point of a bayonet. Many were arrested without being charged with any crime. Debs defied the injunction and continued to lead the strike. He was arrested and sent to a rat-infested jail for several months. In jail, he wrote perhaps the lines he is most famous for:

> While there is a lower class, I am in it.
> While there is a criminal element, I am of it.
> While there is a soul in prison, I am not free.

With Debs in jail and the army in control, the strike was broken and his men returned to work—those who were taken back by the railroads. However, they were forced to sign a pledge that they would never join a union as long as they worked for a railroad. The Pullman workers also returned to the misery that awaited them. The time had not yet arrived when workers would win their struggle for a living wage. They would have to wait until the twentieth century before they could exercise their right to organize, and win decent wages and working conditions.

Texas train wreck, 1918. The arrow points to the body of the engineer in his cab.

11
Safety Comes
to the Railroad

"It was taken as a matter of course that railroad men were to be maimed and killed"

Despite the revolutionary impact of the railroads on nineteenth-century America, in some ways the railroads themselves were extremely conservative. Progress came slowly and at times painfully, and the train itself remained a somewhat primitive machine for almost fifty years. Railroad owners generally did not like to add improvements, for they believed these would add to costs. And sometimes, employees were too stubborn or ignorant to accept new ways of doing things.

One early example of this struggle for change was the development of a signal system between the conductor and the engineer to stop and start the train. Because the first trains lacked a mechanical or electric means of communication between the passenger cars and the locomotive, the conductor could not signal the engineer without getting off the train. He had to descend the train and swing a lantern or call out to let the engineer know if the passengers had boarded. And if the conductor needed to stop the train suddenly, he had to climb into the locomotive cabin while the train was moving to let the engineer know there was a problem.

A conductor named Ayres came up with the simple idea of running a long piece of rope through the passenger cars to the cab of the engine. At the end of the twine he attached a wooden block. Ayres told the engineer that whenever he pulled the twine, the block would jump in the cab and the engineer should stop the train. The only problem was that the engineer, whose name was Hammond, felt himself to be the captain of the train: He wasn't going to take any orders from a lowly conductor. So every time Ayres pulled his cord, the engineer ignored the signal. Ayres was furious. He raced to the locomotive, yanked Hammond out of his cab, and told him that he meant to fight him then and there and that whoever won was going to determine when the train stopped. The fight was short. Ayres whipped the engineer, who, from that moment on, moved according to Ayres's signal. Ayres's system was quickly improved upon and within a short time, a signal system between the conductor and engineer became a standard part of every train.

Another technological development that helped revolutionize the railroad system was the use of the telegraph to coordinate the movements of trains. Until 1850, there was no way of knowing whether or not a train was on schedule once it left the station. If for some reason there was a delay, nobody knew why the train was late or where it was. To avoid an accident, all the trains on that line would be held up. Trains sometimes had to wait for hours on a siding for another train to pass before they could proceed.

On October 22, 1851, Charles Minot, superintendent of the Erie Railroad, single-handedly put an end to this inefficient system. He was on a train headed west that was supposed to meet and then pass an eastbound train. Minot's train arrived at the meeting spot on time, but after an hour's wait, the other train had not arrived. Since there was only a single track, the westbound train could not depart for fear that it would collide with the eastbound train. Minot then walked to the local telegraph office and wired ahead to the next station asking if the eastbound train had passed yet. When he received a reply that it hadn't, he then sent the first telegraph train order in America. "Hold eastbound train until further orders." Minot returned to his train to proceed, but the engineer was unwilling to move ahead based solely on a telegraph wire. Minot then took over the controls himself and drove the train to its destination without incident. From that time on, the telegraph became *the* means to coordinate train movements and schedules. Wherever tracks were built, a telegraph line was built right alongside.

As soon as the telegraph was used to regulate train movements, the number of accidents decreased. Now when a train was running late, other trains could be notified and either move or wait as was needed. But there were always a few people who, like the stubborn engineer Hammond, were too pigheaded to accept new technology. One such man was Jeremiah Preston, the superintendent of the Eastern Railroad, which ran trains between Boston, Massachusetts, and Portland, Maine. He was so stubborn in his refusal to use the telegraph that a passenger train sat at a station all night waiting for a freight to pass while the freight sat in its station all night waiting for the passenger train to pass. A simple telegram could have solved the problem in seconds, but Preston refused to use the telegraph.

On August 26, 1871, the inevitable tragedy happened. The day was miserably hot and thousands of Bostonians were trying to flee the city to the cooler regions of Maine. Three northbound trains followed one another out of the Boston station, heading north to Maine. Two of these trains were scheduled to turn off at the Everett,

Massachusetts, station and take another route. The third train was scheduled to make local stops on the main line to Portland. It was to be followed by the Portland express an hour later.

However, at Everett, the first three trains had to stop and wait for a southbound train that was due to pass before they could proceed. Since the Eastern Railroad refused to use the telegraph, no one knew that the southbound train was an hour and a half late. The three trains just had to wait until the southbound train arrived. As they were waiting, the express train left Boston and headed down the line, its engineer not knowing there were three trains on the tracks ahead of it. As the express raced down the tracks to make up for lost time, the southbound train finally arrived and two of the three trains that were waiting turned off onto another line. But the third train continued on the main line, unaware that the express train was bearing down on it. The night was dark, and a light fog had drifted in from the sea. On the last car of the local, two dim red lights glowed so faintly in the mist that they could not be seen from a distance. When the local train stopped at the town of Revere to pick up and discharge passengers, the Portland express crashed into its rear. Twenty-nine passengers died that night.

New England was in an uproar. Wendell Phillips, one of the most radical public figures of the day, called the accident "deliberate murder." Superintendent Preston denied that the accident could have been prevented by the simple act of sending a telegram, despite the evidence against him. The press carried out an unrelenting crusade against the railroad, until its president and Preston eventually resigned. Within a short time, every New England railroad was using the telegraph.

As bad as most railroads were concerning passenger safety, they were even more negligent about their own crews. The two most dangerous jobs in the railroad were linking cars together and braking.

Safety Comes to the Railroad

For years, the common method of joining one railway car to another was by the pin-and-link system. This required a yardman to stand between the two cars while the locomotive slowly backed up to bring the cars near enough to one another for him to link them. The yardman had to deftly slip a pin on the moving car into the link of the stationary one and then get out of the way quickly. If he failed to do so, he could be crushed to death between the two cars or, at best, only lose a finger or hand.

An equally dangerous job was braking a train. The brakeman had to stop each car individually by tightening a wheel that would lock the brakes. In freight trains, the wheel was on the top of the car so that the brakeman had to stand on top while the train was in motion and turn the wheel. Many brakemen slipped and fell to their deaths, especially in rainy weather when the roof was slippery and visibility poor.

In the early days of railroads, only this primitive technology for linking and braking cars was available. But after the Civil War, two men invented devices that would make such risks unnecessary. One was Eli Hamilton Janney, who invented the automatic coupler that allowed train cars to be joined together without the yardman's having to stand between them. The coupling system could be controlled with a lever operated from outside the cars rather than between them. The other inventor was George Westinghouse, who devised an air brake that could be operated from inside the locomotive, using air pressure to lock the brakes throughout the entire train. Both men demonstrated that their inventions could save thousands of lives. Yet instead of quickly adopting these devices, the railroads ignored them. "Too costly," one railroad executive said, dismissing the matter and, at the same time, expressing the common attitude of most owners. As a result, men continued to be maimed and killed.

This drawing illustrates how the old pin-and-link system worked. It is easy to see how the brakeman could have lost his fingers or his life when the train shifted back and forth as he tried to join the two units.

Safety Comes to the Railroad

The man who was destined to change all this had the unlikely name of Lorenzo Coffin, a prosperous farmer who became a crusader for railroad safety. Coffin was traveling on a train one day when he observed an accident at a station while the train he was riding on was stopped. As two cars were being linked together by the pin-and-link system, a brakeman lost the two remaining fingers of one hand. Coffin was shocked to learn that the man had lost the other fingers in the same way. He was then told how brakemen lost their lives trying to brake trains from the top of a moving freight car during bad weather. But what horrified Coffin more was discovering that Janney and Westinghouse had invented the automatic coupling system and air brakes and that railroads refused to use them. Coffin's crusade began.

> My first job was to arouse the public to this awful wrong, this butchering of these faithful men who were serving the people at such fearful risk of life and limb. Why I had discovered that it was taken as a *matter of course* that railroad men would of necessity be maimed and killed.

At first, Coffin was a prophet without an audience. Whenever he went to see railroad men, they listened to him politely at first, then explained the economics of the business. When he continued to press his case for safety, they ignored him and refused him an audience. Coffin then turned to the press but found that many editors were on railroad payrolls. They threw his articles in the wastepaper basket. When Coffin appeared at state legislatures to plead his case for railway safety, the legislators, most of whom accepted railroad bribes on a regular basis, paid no attention to him. Finally, he turned to small religious papers and farmers' journals to print his articles and bring his case to the people. He described how some 30,000 men had been injured or killed by primitive devices that the railroads refused to abandon. He described what their deaths and injuries did to their families. He drew vivid pictures in print of how a brakeman would stand on top of a fast-moving train during a snowstorm, the freezing wind bearing down on him, blinded by snow, the car he was standing on rocking and swaying as he tried to turn the wheel with frozen hands. And Coffin told what happened if the brakeman slipped and fell between the moving cars. The problem was, as another writer had pointed out, "that as long as brakes cost more than trainmen, trainmen will be sacrificed to the greed of the railroad."

In 1883, at the age of sixty, Coffin was appointed the first railroad commissioner of the state of Iowa. It was a job with little more than a title, but it gave Coffin a platform to gain a wider audience. He continued to write letters and attend conventions—with the same result: Nobody paid any attention to him. Finally, Coffin tried another way. He went to the organization of the companies that built railway cars, the Master Car Builders Association, and proposed that they test Westinghouse's brakes on a long freight train. While everyone agreed that air brakes would work on short, light trains, most railroad workers were positive the brakes would not work on long, heavy freights. But they agreed to the test.

In 1886, seventeen years after they had been invented, the first air brakes were tested on a freight train. They failed to work. Another test was made and again the brakes failed. Coffin was ridiculed. But Westinghouse himself had been present at the second test. He immediately began working on a solution to the brake problem. One year later, on a steep stretch of track in Burlington, Iowa, a freight train came down the grade at forty miles an hour, a high rate of speed for those days. As a test, the signal was given and the engineer applied Westinghouse's air brakes. To everyone's astonishment, the train came to a smooth stop within five hundred feet. The only sound was the hissing of compressed air. Coffin began to cry. "I am the happiest man in all Creation," he said.

Coffin still had some distance to go before his dream would come true. First, he wrote a railway safety law for the state of Iowa, requiring trains to use both air brakes and automatic couplers. The law was passed, but the railways ignored it. He then wrote a bill requiring that all railroads use air brakes and submitted it to the U.S. Congress. Congress refused to consider the bill, although everyone agreed it was a worthwhile piece of legislation. The railroads still had too much power and influence and they were able to block it. Finally, in 1893, almost twenty years after Coffin began his crusade, Congress finally reversed itself and adopted his bill, and the president signed it into law. As soon as the railroads began to adopt the new safety features, with much complaining and grumbling, accident rates dropped 60 percent for crews and almost 100 percent for passengers. The ultimate irony was that the railroads liked the safety features so much that they began to improve upon them. Soon they were boasting of the safety features of their trains as if they, and not Janney, Westinghouse, and Coffin, had made these safety devices a reality.

Another change that saved passengers' lives was the use of steam instead of stoves to provide heat for passenger cars. Whenever a train had an accident and there were stoves on board, the hot embers started fires. Many people who were trapped but survived the crash were burned to death. The use of steam heat put an end to this.

Yet, even with safety devices, trains still had accidents. By 1890, 6,335 people had died in train wrecks and 29,000 had been injured. Part of the problem was that improvements in railroad technology increased the speed and weight of trains. While the first trains averaged fifteen to twenty miles an hour, by 1890 trains were reaching speeds of a hundred miles an hour. And the faster and heavier the trains were, the greater the loss of life during an accident. One railroad company, the Lake Shore and Michigan, was warned that one of its bridges in Ashtabula, Ohio, was not strong enough to support a train. Charles Collins, the chief mechanical engineer of the railroad, indignantly insisted that nothing was wrong with the bridge. The next week as the train passed over the level bridge, the locomotive engineer suddenly felt as if he were traveling uphill. He was. The bridge was suddenly sagging under the weight of the train, and the front end rose as the rear end fell. The engineer opened the throttle, hoping to race the train across the bridge before it collapsed. The engine snapped free of the cars behind it and made it across, but the passenger cars plunged into the icy river below; the parts not submerged caught fire. Eighty-three people were killed. When Collins learned of the tragedy, he went home, shut the door of his study, and shot himself. Five years later, the former president of the line, Amasa Stone, who had been depressed ever since the accident happened, also committed suicide.

Such a reaction was rare. Most railroads were not held responsible for accidents, and their executives seldom felt guilty about them, even if there was gross negligence on the railroad's part. One newspaper, outraged by this, published an angry editorial:

> A train thunders down a curve . . . a rail snaps . . . two cars are hurled off a bank, six or seven corpses and a score of injured victims taken from the ruins, and nobody is to blame. Nobody ever is. . . . Boilers are bursting all over the country, railroad bridges breaking, rails slipping, human life is squandered . . . but nobody is to blame.

John Quincy Adams, the sixth president of the United States, had once been in a train wreck and never forgot it. He wrote in his diary:

> Of the 16 persons in the car that overturned, only one escaped [being] hurt. One man was so badly mangled, he died within ten minutes. Men, women and children were scattered along the road, bleeding, mangled, groaning, writhing in torture and dying.

There was nothing more gruesome than a train wreck. And more often than not, wrecks were caused by negligence or poor judgment. One tragic example of this was the train accident that occurred at Ivanhoe, Indiana, in 1918. A circus company had just finished its performance in Ivanhoe and had boarded a train headed for the town of Hammond. On board were three hundred acrobats, aerialists, strongmen, clowns, animal trainers, horseback riders, and the "100 Famous Dancing Girls," a troupe of ballet dancers. As the train headed toward its next destination in the early hours of the morning, most of the performers were sleeping. The conductor thought he smelled something burning—like a piece of equipment overheating. He ordered the engineer to stop the train while he got out and inspected. As soon as the train stopped two automatic signals were set to warn any oncoming train that there was another train stalled on the tracks ahead of it and that it should stop. In addition, as an extra safety precaution, the conductor sent a flagman to the rear of the train with a bright lantern to flag down any train that might approach. However, it was unthinkable that any engineer would miss two automatic stop signals.

As the conductor was inspecting the problem, the flagman could see the bright headlight of an approaching train. He was startled when it failed to stop at the first automatic signal and horrified to see it rush past the second. The flagman frantically waved his lantern to signal the engineer of the oncoming train to put on the brakes, but the engineer barreled past him and into the rear of the stalled circus train.

The Iron Horse

It was one of the most terrifying accidents in railroad history. The train smashed through the four sleeping cars, crushing and mangling hundreds of circus people. Hercules, the circus strongman, was crushed to death along with the famed Romey family of bareback riders and Rose Borland, then the world's most famous horseback rider. Of the "100 Famous Dancing Girls," more than twenty were killed. What made the tragedy even worse was that the old wooden cars in which the circus performers were sleeping caught fire when the gas tanks used to supply fuel for lamplight exploded and set fire to the cars. Townspeople desperately tried to rescue the passengers, but there was no water nearby and they had to stand by helplessly while people who might have been saved were burned to death. Leon Moore, a clown, was one of those pulled from the wreck:

> I was asleep and the crash awakened me. I realized the car was being destroyed. I grabbed a pillow and put it over my face. I felt myself being drawn into a knot. When I came to myself, I had the body of a naked person over me—a corpse. Then I heard an awful cry—"the fire's coming." But my best pal, Emil Swire, stuck with me although the flames were hot around him and I was saved.

By the time the fires burned themselves out, sixty-eight circus performers were dead and 147 injured. At a hearing held several days later to determine the cause of the accident, the engineer of the oncoming train, who escaped with minor injuries, confessed that he had had "little or no sleep the previous 24 hours" and had eaten several heavy meals. To make matters worse, he had taken what were called in those days kidney pills, which contained narcotics and made him sleepy. He said the reason he never saw the signals was that he

Drawing of Kate Shelley showing how she crossed the bridge during a storm to warn an oncoming train of danger ahead.

had fallen asleep at the throttle of his train and only woke up a moment before he crashed into the circus car.

There were many tales of heroism to match the tragedies. A famous railroad heroine who prevented an accident was Kate Shelley, who one night was watching a railroad crew testing a bridge on the outskirts of Chicago in the middle of a storm. As they were working on the bridge, it collapsed and the crew was swept into the river. Two men were carried away and two hung on for dear life. Shelley knew that in a short time an express train with hundreds of passengers aboard was due to pass over the bridge. She had to get the train station to tell the stationmaster to flag the train down. But to do that she had to cross over another railroad bridge in the storm. She took a kerosene lamp with her, but as she started to cross the bridge, the wind blew the lamp out and she had to cross in the dark, with howling winds and driving rain beating down on her. One false step would have plunged her into the raging river below. Step by step she inched forward until she finally made it across and then raced to the station, where she warned the stationmaster. He stopped the train and sent out a rescue crew to save the two men, who were still alive when they arrived.

Another accident was prevented by a sharpshooting freight conductor by the name of Charles Watlington. Watlington was a veteran of the railroad wars that broke out from time to time when two lines were competing for the same route. Gangs were hired to beat up and even shoot each other, and railroad employees had to learn how to use a gun and use it well.

Watlington was working on a freight train that was forced to stop when a storm washed out the tracks in front of it. Knowing that a passenger train was not far behind him, Watlington took a red lantern to flag it down so as to prevent it from crashing into the rear of the stalled freight. It was dark and rainy, and as the passenger train approached Watlington, the engineer did not see him signaling to stop. As the train raced by, Watlington reached for his pistol and, taking aim, fired at the air hose between the last two passenger cars. It was a good or lucky shot, for he hit the target and severed the hose, setting the brakes in action and bringing the train to a stop.

Perhaps the most famous locomotive engineer of all was Casey Jones, who sacrificed his life in 1900 to save his crew and passengers. Casey was driving the Cannonball Express and was behind schedule by almost two hours. Vowing to make up the lost time, he opened the throttle wide and raced the train at a hundred miles an hour—an extraordinarily high speed in those days. He was almost back on schedule when he approached Vaughn, Mississippi. A crew was on the tracks frantically trying to switch a freight train onto a side track so that the Cannonball Express could pass. An air hose had ruptured and one of the cars was stuck. The crew was still desperately trying to remove the train when the Cannonball Express rushed out of the night and fog, headed right at the stalled train. Casey realized there was no time to stop the train. He yelled for his crew to jump, then threw the locomotive in reverse, using every skill he had to lessen the impact of the collision. He was fully aware that he didn't have a chance of surviving but hoped that his actions might save the lives of others. The Cannonball crashed into the rear of the freight, smashing through the last cars, tossing produce sky-high, and spinning around so that it faced in the opposite direction from which it came. Casey was killed, but everyone else was saved. A song was written to honor him, and he became the most famous locomotive engineer of the time.

Picture of Casey Jones taken in the cab of his train about a year before he

heroically lost his life in a train wreck.

The Iron Horse

It was bad enough that trains had unexpected or unintended crashes. But one of the most famous accidents in the nineteenth century was deliberate. It was actually a publicity stunt that unexpectedly turned into a tragedy.

The Great Texas Train Crash of 1896, as it was called, was the invention of a man whose name, appropriately enough, was G. W. Crush, an agent for the Katy Railroad. Business must have been slow for Crush to come up with his brainstorm—to stage a "Monster Railroad Wreck" in Waco, Texas, and sell tickets to the event. His idea was to take two old locomotives no longer in use, attach six out-of-date passenger cars to them, and run them into each other at high speed.

Crush began to advertise in newspapers throughout Texas, Kansas, and the Indian Territory (now part of Oklahoma). Agents for the railroads put up posters everywhere announcing the Great Train Crash. At the same time, Crush built huge concession stands where food and lemonade could be sold, adding to the railroad's profits.

Crush was wrong about one thing. He expected 20,000 people to attend; 30,000 showed up. They came on special excursion trains set up by the railroad from as far as hundreds of miles away. It was a great picnic and everybody was in a festive mood for the event. At four o'clock in the afternoon, two locomotives were brought out and shown to the crowd and then backed up so that they would be several miles apart. At five o'clock, the signal was given for the event to start. A reporter for the *Dallas Morning News* described what happened next:

> The rumble of the two trains, faint and far off at first, but growing nearer and more distinct with each flitting second, was like the gathering of a cyclone. Nearer and nearer they

came. . . . Every eye was strained. Every nerve on edge.
They rolled down at a frightful speed [sixty miles an hour]
and hundreds who had come miles to see them found their
hearts growing faint and were compelled to turn away. . . .
Words bend and break in an attempt to describe it. It was a
scene that will haunt many a man. . . . A crash, a sound of
timbers torn and rent and then a show of splinters. Then
followed a swift silence. Then the boilers exploded and the
air was filled with flying missiles from the size of a postage
stamp to half a drive wheel falling indiscriminately on the
just and the unjust, the poor and the rich, great and small.

The two engines went right through each other. A smokestack
landed a quarter of a mile away. A farmer who fell out of a tree and
broke his leg was one of the lucky ones. Flying pieces of timber and
chunks of metal killed and injured many. That didn't ruin the festivi-
ties, though. People continued to drink and eat, satisfied they had
witnessed the single greatest spectacle of the nineteenth century as
ambulances carried the dead, dying, and injured away. The Great
Texas Train Crash symbolized much of what nineteenth-century
railroads were about.

As the twentieth century began, the railroads began to show
increasing concern for the safety of both their passengers and their
workmen. Accidents were more the result of human error than
technical failure as the railroads incorporated the latest technological
advances to minimize collisions. Yet technology has its limitations,
and even today, almost 150 years after the first train wreck, railway
accidents still occur, with an occasional great loss of life and many
injuries.

A typical late-nineteenth-century scene: freight train passing through town.

12
Conclusion

"The magnificent blessing of the railroad is sometimes turned into a curse"

The railroads were a mixed blessing for America. They created much that was good and brought about much that was harmful. On one hand, they transformed America from a collection of isolated rural communities into a unified nation. They linked village to village and town to town—and eventually, ocean to ocean. The railroads created new towns and brought prosperity to cities. They provided Americans with their first fast, relatively efficient means of travel. Their power to transport goods created markets that made possible large-scale industrial and agricultural production. On the other hand, they ended the solitary rural life of many Americans and the rich cultures of Native American tribes. They contributed to the destruction of the Western prairie and the buffalo. The robber barons who created railroad empires often did so by stealing millions, corrupting politicians, extorting farmers and merchants, and exploiting their own workers. This contradictory nature of the railroad caused Tom Watson, a southern political leader, to remark that "the magnificent blessing of the railroad is sometimes turned into a curse."

The Iron Horse

But for the average nineteenth-century American who was not brutalized by railroad policies, trains were poetry set to motion. Even their names sounded to many like poems—the Atchison, Topeka & Santa Fe; the Chesapeake and Ohio; the Delaware and Lackawanna. A train was a symbol of power, speed, and glamour, a mechanical magic carpet that whisked people through an ever-changing landscape that ranged from peaceful farms to roaring cities to awesome mountains to terrifying deserts. In many ways, the railroad *was* the nineteenth century.

But eventually, the almost unlimited power of the railroad barons was checked by a number of forces. The anger of the American people at the railroaders' arrogance and devious ways brought about changes in laws that gave the U.S. government power to regulate rates and the sale of railroad stocks and bonds. Workers began to successfully demand and receive decent wages and hours. New means of transportation, including the automobile, truck, and airplane, competed for both passengers and freight.

The railroads responded to these new challenges with new technologies that provided faster, safer, and more comfortable travel. Diesel and electric power replaced steam. Trains now travel at speeds of two hundred miles an hour and faster. Yet despite their efficiency and comfort, and the great technological advances today's railroads have made over those of the past, they lack the romantic appeal that once enchanted Americans. For almost a hundred years, they carried out a ritual that was a kind of bonding between them and the railroad. They gathered on hilltops, in fields, and along lonely country roads to wait for the train to pass by. They were thrilled by the roar of its powerful engine, by the high, piercing shriek of its whistle, and, most of all, by the chance to wave and be waved at by the man whom they considered to be the most extraordinary and lucky human being on the face of the earth—the locomotive engineer.

Glossary of Railroad Terms

air monkey	*air brake repairman*
blind	*space between locomotive and baggage car*
boomer	*hobo who travels around and works on the railroad*
conder dick	*railroad detective*
crummy	*caboose*
deadhead	*passenger riding free*
gandy dancer	*track laborer*
gate	*switch*
green eye	*clear signal*
hog	*locomotive*
hogger	*engineer*
highball	*clear signal/fast run*
railroad bull	*railroad cop*
red ball	*fast freight*
reefer	*refrigerator car*
rattler	*freight train*
scab	*strike breaker; worker hired to replace one who is on strike*
shack	*brakeman*
snake	*switcher*
yegg	*thief*

Bibliography

Brown, Dee Alexander. *Hear That Lonesome Whistle Blow*. New York: Holt, Rinehart and Winston, 1975.

————, and Martin F. Schmidt. *Fighting Indians of America*. New York: Bonanza, 1958.

Fisher, Leonard Everett. *Tracks Across America*. New York: Holiday House, 1992.

Griswold, Wesley. *Train Wreck*. Brattleboro, Vt.: Stephen Greene Press, 1969.

Holbrook, Stewart. *The Story of the American Railroad*. New York: Crown, 1947.

Horan, James D. *The Pinkertons: The Detective Dynasty That Made America*. New York: Bonanza, 1957.

Jefferis, David. *Trains: The History of Railroads*. New York: Franklin Watts, 1991.

Jensen, Oliver. *The American Heritage History of Railroads*. New York: American Heritage, 1975.

Josephson, Matthew. *The Robber Barons*. New York: Harcourt, Brace and Co., 1962.

Lewis, Oscar. *The Big Four*. New York: Alfred A. Knopf, 1938.

————. *Sea Routes to the Gold Field*. New York: Alfred A. Knopf, 1949.

McKissack, Patricia and Frederick. *A Long Hard Journey*. New York: Walker and Company, 1990.

Miller, Marilyn. *The Transcontinental Railroad*. Morristown, N.J.: Silver Burdett Press, 1985.

Bibliography

Smith, Page. *The Rise of Industrial America: A People's History of the Reconstruction Era*. New York: McGraw-Hill, 1984.

Stone, Irving. *Men to Match My Mountains*. New York: Doubleday, 1956.

Turner, George. *Victory Rode the Rails: The Strategic Place of Railroads in the Civil War*. Indianapolis: Bobbs-Merrill, 1953.

Wormser, Richard L. *Pinkerton: America's First Private Eye*. New York: Walker and Company, 1989.

Index

Note: Page numbers in italics refer to illustrations.

Index

Index

Index

Index

Index

Steam engine, 6, 110
Steam locomotive, 1–2, 9–10
Steamboat, 6–9, *8*, 33, 43, 113
Stevens, John, 9
Stevenson, Robert Louis, 124
Stock(s) (railroad), 25–26, 58
    "watering," 24
Stock speculators, 16, 17
Stokes, Ed, 28
Stone, Amasa, 160
Strikes, 138–43, *139*, 145
Sundance Kid, 92
Supreme Court, 115, 116, 130, 131,
    148

Tall Bull (Cheyenne chief), 76
Technology, 159–60, 169, 172
    and safety, 151–59
Telegraph, 152–54
Thompson, Willie, 74
Thoreau, Henry, 17, 108
Time zones, 108, *109*
Track, 30
    laying, for transcontinental rail-
        road, *61*, 62, 69, 78, 81, 83
    miles of, 10, 17, 47–48, 97, 100
Tom Thumb (steam locomotive), 1–2
Train robbery(ies), 85–95, 116–19
Train stations, 106
Train wrecks, *150*, 160–61
    see also Accidents
Trains
    express, *96*
    speed and weight of, 159–60
Transcontinental railroad, 31, 40, 44–
    45, 100
    grading, *63*

joining east and west tracks of, *82*
    race to build, 62–83
    uniting America, *56*, 57–83
Transportation revolution, 2–3, 97
Turnpikes, 3
Twain, Mark, 9, 33–35

Unemployment, 137, 145
Union Pacific (railroad), 58–59, 62,
    72–74, 76–77, 78, 81–83, *82*, 111,
    123–24
    laying track for, *61*
Unions, 137–41, 143–49
U.S. Army, 74–76, 78
Utah, 58, 59, 81

Vanderbilt, Cornelius, *18*, 20–22, 25–
    28
Vigilantes, 87, 88–89
Villard, Henry, 100

Wages, 111, 137, 147, 149
Wagon trains, *5*
Wagons, 2, 3, 4
Warfare, railroads in, 47–55, *52*
Watlington, Charles, 164–65
Watson, Tom, 171
West (the), 43, 100–102
Westinghouse, George, 155, 157, 158,
    159
Workers, 131, 172
    organization of, 137–41, 143–49
    revolt by, 133–49
    and safety, 154–59

Yellow fever, 40, 41, 60
Younger, Cole, 89